Good Grief!

ALSO BY ELLEN STIMSON

Mud Season

Good Grief!

Life in a Tiny Vermont Village

Ellen Stimson

THE COUNTRYMAN PRESS
Woodstock, Vermont

Book design and composition by Eugenie S. Delaney

Published by The Countryman Press, P.O. Box 748, Woodstock, VT 05091
Distributed by W. W. Norton & Company, Inc., 500 Fifth Avenue,
New York, NY 10110
Printed in the United States of America

10 9 8 7 6 5 4 3 2 1

Library of Congress Cataloging-in-Publication Data are available

Good Grief!
978-1-58157-255-1

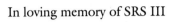

In loving memory of SRS III

Contents

Prologue

I'VE ALWAYS BELIEVED THAT ONE OF THE GREAT REASONS TO be alive is that we don't know what's coming around the next corner. We don't know what grand passions are going to take over and change everything. I always knew I wanted kids. Of course, I had no idea what that would really be like. No one does. People dreaming about having kids never say, "Oh, honey, let's have a teenager!" There's a good reason for that.

We are a family of five, mostly. My husband, John, and I have three kids: Benjamin, Hannah, and Eli. Before that, I was married for what seemed like about fifteen minutes to Benjamin's dad, Steve, so he has always been part of our crew, too. But if you start adding in all the folks that are, or seem like, family, the list gets a bit long. It takes a village. My oldest friend, Cheska, used to say that our holidays, with past and present husbands, current in-laws, former in-laws, and dearest friends, were a bit like an Alan Alda movie. Now, just imagine the weddings and the funerals.

Our family defines me. For John and me, "parenting" really is a verb. It is an active part of our lives, even now that two of our kids are ostensibly all grown up. Our philosophy has mainly been to love them up, have lots of experiences together, then follow their lead and see what happens. And believe me, there has always been plenty to see.

These days, the kids are fishing for tuna off the coast of Martha's Vineyard, raising a Great Dane puppy in a tiny sixth-floor walkup, and chopping wood in a sustainable mountain community. They live by the water, on a mountain, and in the middle of Manhattan.

And here's the thing. We're also getting older. We're growing up. All of us. Surprisingly, as it turns out, there is almost as much parenting at this stage as there was at any other. At this point, we are supposed to be teaching them how to choose a career, how to be a good neighbor, how to deal with life's unexpected challenges, and maybe most importantly of all, how to choose a life partner. I guess we have been working on these all along, only now (when the kids occasionally decide to date, umm . . . let's just say people you might imagine in a police lineup) the lessons seem more urgent. Some of these lessons weren't at all what we imagined we'd be learning and teaching at this stage. But life has a way of altering your plans.

A few years ago, we managed to go pretty well broke on an old country store,[1] where we developed a positive genius for doing everything wrong. That little store, tucked away in the mountains, had looked sweet, charming, and not at all like the kind of thing that could completely ruin you. Now, there was a story with plenty of lessons to go around.

But so long as we can build a fire, make a comforting meal, and gather together at the table with our chosen family, I know we're in the right place. Besides, let me tell you , this family is growing up and out. We are learning new stuff. Big, important stuff.[2] And making new stories practically faster than I can write them down.

Ellen Stimson

Dorset, Vermont

---

1. That store (aka Peltier's, aka the Horrible Quaint Country Store) was the quirky focus of *Mud Season,* a book about the beauty of Vermont and a few minor, little, hardly worth mentioning, really, misadventures that we got up to when we first moved up here.

2. When I was younger, looking ahead, I figured that by now we'd be done with all of that learning. I thought we'd pretty well know all about the big stuff. I mean, I'd had a few existential crises. I did therapy. But, no. Turns out, you are never done.

CHAPTER ONE

At the Table

Food can fix almost anything. That is practically a sacred canon around our house. We make cupcakes for the kids on Sunday night and they feel loved come Monday when they find one in their lunch. Unrelenting snowstorms? Easy. I slow-cook braised ribs in a deep, rich, winy sauce with onions, garlic, a little cayenne pepper, some tarragon, and dark chocolate. The house smells warm and we feel full and happy. The snow will almost seem like a comfort. Lonely? Well, then I bake bread. Just the smell of baking bread is good company. It will travel on the air. Pretty soon someone will come along looking for a bite.

Food comforts and brings joy. When you are falling in love, feeding each other chocolate-dipped strawberries seems to be an almost universal desire. We honor milestones with champagne, which goes even better with salty almonds and blue cheese. Food is ritual and sustenance. Obviously, I have thought a lot about this.

Living in the mountains of Vermont, where the restaurant choices are especially few after nine o'clock, means a lot of entertaining, with long, complicated meals. John baked his grandmother's bread recipe for me one Christmas shortly after we met, and I married him for it. Well, mostly for the bread. Now, he and I have been cooking side by side for twenty-five years. So we've had lots of practice. And everyone says we are good cooks. They are, as it turns out, right. John likes to read recipes with interesting grills and marinades, and he makes big, happy pastas. I like to blend deep flavors, bake lots of doughy things, and create a table where laughter and solace are on offer. This whole eating and cooking thing is something I totally know how to do. So that's why discovering that I never "properly" learned how to use a knife and fork came as such a surprise.

My daughter, Hannah, was newly dating Dan Lewis. Dan is the delightful son of Anette, a stylish, German-born, film-producing New Yorker, and Bob, her charming southern finance-guy husband. Apparently, the Lewis family eats in a more European style than we do.

Hannah was home having dinner with us one weekend when she started in. Some kids come home from college peddling transcendental meditation. Or veganism. Maybe liberation theology. But Hannah decided that the battle she would bring to me was over the use of eating utensils.

"*Mo-mmm*. Look, it's not hard. You don't have to grip that fork like I was trying to take it away from you. Dan's parents eat so much more . . . elegantly."

I, of course, responded like any sane person would. "What?"

She explained. "Mom, you're just holding that fork in your right hand and using it for everything. You're sawing away at the meat and then scooping up bites."

Well, yeah. "And your point is?"

"Look, Mom. If you hold the fork in your left hand and your knife in your right hand, you can cut and eat all at the same time. There's no reason to put down the knife. You just use both hands. It only takes practice to eat left-handed."

According to my girl, while I was using my fork for nearly everything, the Lewis's knives were settled in right hands while forks gently floated around in their left. To hear her describe it, they may as well have been doing dinner ballet.

Now, of course, these were not the first people I had ever observed picking up their knives practically before anything else. You know, I am not a complete rube. I have traveled widely and I have eaten well in all of those places. And I've been to Europe, for God's sakes. Hannah, though, seemed to have just noticed our thoroughly American eating habits, with the not-so-quiet disdain of the very young adult. She had quickly mastered the art of the knife, and she wondered whyever we couldn't manage it, too.

She was convinced this style was prettier. Perhaps it felt more genteel. Maybe the appeal was that it was exotic, since we didn't eat that way. Whatever. She brought this up at five dinners in a damned row after that. It was becoming an issue.

Now, you may not know this, but I am not known for my great coordination or grace. No one has ever said, "Oh, Ellen? She glides through the room."

My artistic talent is limited to your basic first-grader stick figures, and if I were asked to take the roadside DUI test, I would surely fail, at 9:00 AM, stone-cold sober, any day of the week. Straight lines and I do not mix. I mean, we've met. We're just not on a first-name basis. My left hand might as well not even be there, for all the good it does me. So the notion of holding a fork (upside down) and feeding myself with that stranger of a hand just seemed silly.

Hannah asserted that "It just takes a little practice, Mom. Watch."

I watched her. Okay, I admit it was, actually, prettier. But I've never really had a talent for alternate eating utensils. Like chopsticks, for instance. I never really mastered chopsticks. With the exception of the easiest foods, I hardly even try to pretend. It's not comfortable. And more importantly, I'm not very good at it. Besides, we're talking about dinner here, not a DUI test. Do I really want to make it any more difficult than it has to be?

Still, she had planted the seed.

One gorgeous, sunny afternoon, I found myself with a couple

of my isabelpratt[1] clients at Pastis, in New York City. Pastis is one of the Keith McNally spots. He is best known for the flagship Balthazar, but Pastis is my favorite. They have the finest steak tartare in the city, and the steak frites are just about a perfect food. The oysters are always fresh and the mignonette sauce is an ideal blend of vinegar with garlic, onion, and maybe just a touch of sweet sherry. On late spring and early fall days, the sidewalk tables are full of half-drunken, blissed-out diners. I might be one of them, actually, if you find yourself passing by. And if I seem a little teary? Well, they have a Beaujolais that can make me cry.

So we were a little overdressed for the sidewalk, but we were enjoying an exquisite Indian-summer day. The morning had been chilly, but the late-afternoon sunshine made it plenty warm enough to sit outside. Stewart and his wife, Melanie, had joined me to celebrate the new high school they'd just opened. They run the Greenwood School in Putney, Vermont. Greenwood is a destination for boys with learning differences who have struggled in traditional education models. This school takes kids that are worn out from trying to fit into mainstream institutions and gives them hope. They leave that place tended, loved, and succeeding. Now listen. I seem to think I know everything that there is to know about education. You can just ask me. I'll tell you. So I can tell you that this is the most loving, benevolent place I know. All of this is a long way of saying that Stewart and Melanie and I know each other well. We've worked together for years and I'm comfortable with them.

So there we were, and out came a plate piled high with oysters and sardines, alongside the tartare. There was a basket of frites and a rich béarnaise. There may have been a hint of wine flowing at the

---

1. isabelpratt is the name of my development agency. We help launch and grow ethical community-service organizations. We raise money for schools, colleges, and hospitals mostly.

table. Did I mention the Beaujolais? By the time the entrées actually came out, we were each a little tipsy with the thrill of all this great food. And possibly the Beaujolais. So when our guests, potential donors to the school, picked up their knives and began eating, I thought, Huh? They do it, too. I'd never noticed.

I was feeling so full and so satisfied that I thought, You know, this might be the perfect time to try out Hannah's "better" way to eat. Good food, good friends, and new adventures in utensils.

Hannah was right. It *was* prettier. These folks did look more . . . worldly . . . at the table. I'm fifty years old. How hard could this be?[2]

Next thing you know, I was holding my knife in my right hand and thinking, Now isn't that lovely? So graceful.

I took up the fork left-handed and remembered Hannah's admonition that my pointer[3] should rest horizontally along the top of the now-upside-down fork. I paused for a moment and realized that, by George, I had it. I looked just as elegant as the rest of them.

At that point I'm sure that they must have been saying things . . . having a conversation or something, as I was having this exquisite moment of my own at the table, but I have no idea what that might have been. I mean, look at that left-handed fork grip. That's elegance right there. That's sophistication. Besides, I was too busy giving rapt attention to my knife, as I gingerly cut a bit of steak, to listen in on whatever chatter seemed important. And that cut was perfectly executed, if I do say so myself. A steak has never been cut with quite such panache.

---

2. Why do warning bells never go off when this sentence enters my thoughts? You'd think that I would have learned by now.

3. She did say "pointer," like she was explaining this to a kindergartner. And just then, I was grateful that she had.

I tilted my fork, skewered the bite, and raised it gently toward my mouth, feeling triumphant. Triumphant! Europeans, my ass. Sophisticated? I'll show you sophisticated. I can do this, too. Of course I can.

Only then . . . well, nothing happened.

I had a mouth full of exactly . . . nothing. It took a second to register.

What???

This really doesn't taste like steak. Hmm?

And, of course, I had missed my mouth. Entirely. The fork was now elegantly resting on my cheek, waiting for someone to tell my sophisticated European left hand what to do and where to go next. The steak had flown off to parts unknown. Possibly on the Continent. Possibly somewhere over my shoulder. Or in my hair. Possibly in Melanie's purse. But not in my mouth.

I dropped the knife. Probably the fork, too. I suddenly wondered if there was an appropriately European way to deal with this situation. Maybe Hannah would think there was a prettier way to grab my napkin and laugh in a manic cackle, but you know, delicately . . . into my napkin. Oh my God, I missed my mouth.

This really all started because of the fire.

ooooo

The previous fall, our Hannah was bringing home a boyfriend to meet us[4] and I celebrated, as one does, with a little house fire. Though it was actually fall, I should be clear that I don't mean a nice, autumnal bonfire. No. Equally, this wasn't the kind of fire that clearly requires a call to the fire department. Almost, but not quite. It was a Goldilocks fire, I suppose.

---

4. Not Euro-eating Dan.

Why would I set the house on fire, you might ask? The thing is that the boyfriend was thirteen years older than Hannah. And he was a bum. No, really, an actual bum.

Well, I guess technically he was a ski and surf bum, but still. "Bum" was the word.

Yes, I know. Every girl has that inappropriate boyfriend. Or six. So it shouldn't have been a surprise. Hannah is brilliant. And she is very mature for her age. We'd always been lucky with her romantic attachments. I guess we'd gotten used to her good sense. But then came the bum.

And did I mention older? An older bum. She was twenty-one and he was ninety-seven or something like that. Thirty-four? Well, it certainly may as well have been ninety-seven. Anyway, they'd met the summer before on Martha's Vineyard. She had been nannying as a summer job, and we had vacationed there. She met him while we were on the island, but I was, apparently, not interested in meeting this practically middle-aged dreamboat of hers. I might have said something, in passing, mind you, about there being something not quite right with a man who couldn't attract women his own age. I'm sure I didn't use the phrase "stalking college girls." That would have been indelicate.

My lack of interest didn't seem to deter our girl, though. Supposedly, this guy was handsome. Possibly charming. Grrreat.

For some reason, Hannah thought that I'd want to know all about Jett. Yes, Jett. It rhymes with wet. He could be on a soap opera based on the name alone.

Oddly enough, I simply had no interest. My friend Melanie suggested that it was probably just Hannah's *Eat, Pray, Love* summer. Okay. Yes. That sounded about right. John and I decided to ignore it. We figured it was a summer fling that would pale in the winter months when she was back with her classmates at the all-women's school, where she had solid feminist politics for breakfast. Sometimes lunch and dinner were served with a side of responsibility and a steaming cup of fighting the good fight. A good menu for level heads.

Only then, Jett started talking to her about moving to San Diego. San Diego? Yes, San Diego, a place that Google Maps leads me to believe is as far away from Dorset, Vermont, as you can get without crossing an ocean. Apparently, he was in capital *L* Love. Hannah could make all of his life's mistakes come out right in the end. She was The One. He wanted her to meet his *fucking parents.* Well, shit. The ignoring strategy might not have been so well considered, after all.

We began to wonder if they might elope. Was that a possibility? Was she actually serious about this . . . guy?

We decided to invite Jett to Vermont one weekend for brunch. None of us felt ready to handle an overnight visit, but brunch . . . well, we could do brunch. That's a meal that can't even commit to a time of day. It's not breakfast. It's not lunch. It's brunch. It's casual. You can invite a guy to brunch without having him abscond with your daughter to make her his bride in some mountain cabin to raise his supposedly handsome babies without ever coming home. So, brunch it was. Brunch we could do.

Of course, I had to start really focusing on the issue. I needed to know what I was dealing with. And Hannah happily filled me in.

He lived in Vail during the winter, and then stored his ski gear before heading back to Martha's Vineyard for the summer. A place where he met impressionable, compassionate college girls with suspicious parents.

Also, he could surf and golf. Two skills that Vermont doesn't really call for, but I guess we should all be well-rounded. During the summer, he was a chef. "Chef" is a word which here means waited tables on the island. It wasn't as steady a job as winter in the Ski Shop, but I guess you have to play the hand you're dealt.

At thirty-four (ninety-seven) he'd never been married, or fathered any children. He owned no house, condo, or apartment. He had no car and no pets. But, on the plus side, he skied 110 days per year. Hannah, it should be said, doesn't ski. She doesn't, actually, love cold weather. Sure we live in Vermont, but the snow is not her favorite part. John and I were having a bit of a tough time seeing the attraction. But, you know, it was Hannah that was attracted to this guy. Her parents weren't really important to that. Besides, there must be some appeal we weren't hearing about.

So we did our research. In this day and age, I'm afraid that means we turned to Facebook. Facebook revealed Jett to be handsome in that thin, muscular, heroin-addict sort of way. He also seemed to like cheap beer. Lots of it, if we're to believe the things we saw online.[5] It became pretty clear that Jett's biggest commitment was to snow. Well, at least he wouldn't find Vermont tiresome. We get a lot of snow, after all.

And then I saw his . . . I hesitate to categorize this as support . . . but apparently he was a Republican. A Republican ski bum? Seriously? A Republican ski bum for our politically liberal girl? Well, okay. So let's see. He supported the war in Iraq. It seems clear that the support was on Facebook and not by enlisting or anything, but I guess that's still . . . well, a sort of support. Oh, and it looked like he was planning to vote for McCain-Palin. He likes Palin? Palin? I ask you!

---

5. I was finally finding a use for Facebook, at least. Let's call it a learning experience.

John and I were not amused.

So an October Sunday brunch was the big meeting. We figured we'd better make nice. I mean, just in case this guy fathered our grandchild or something. Hannah was an adult . . . mostly . . . and we could make nice for a morning. I mean, we love our girl. We could at least do that. Only, as it turns out, we aren't so good at making nice. Not so good at all.

I thought that given how much I was dreading this I could at least find something positive to do with it. Cooking, right? I love to cook. I'd just make a little brunch adventure out of the whole thing. So I asked John, "What do you think we should serve? Maybe I can do some of my famous latkes."

My ever-gracious spouse chipped in with, "Sure. Fine. Whatever. Or maybe we could just hard-boil some eggs and leave 'em in a bowl. I mean, Ellen, we do not want to waste much energy on this. Do we?"

John was having a little trouble transitioning out of the "ignoring" strategy. Truth be told, we simply could not imagine what our smart, beautiful, collegiate girl saw in this guy. It was tough for us to make the leap—and leap it was—from closing our eyes with our fingers in our ears chanting, "NYAH NYAH NYAH NYAH NYAH I CAN'T HEAR YOU!" to a strategy of breakfast foods and grace. But it was October. October. It had been five months. And five months was long enough to realize that this wasn't just going to go away. Hannah had always been thoughtful, organized, and careful. There must be something more to this guy if she still liked him after five months. We had to make an effort.

Really.

The dreaded day dawned beautiful and sunny. I went out to the woods and gathered a bunch of beautiful maple leaves for the table. Vermont in the fall means leaves. And so I thought they'd make a nice table decoration. They would seem to have just drifted down from the limbs overhead, somehow missing the roof, but still it would be lovely. And gracious. And I needed things to be lovely and gracious that morning.

I made my latkes and a tomato-basil strata with bacon-wrapped chestnuts alongside. There were eggs en cocotte. There were home-made cheddar biscuits. I might have said that I love to cook. I cook when I am happy, and, now that I mention it, when I am upset. This might have been an upset brunch. Maybe. There were piles of food everywhere, all on the verge of readiness. Who knows? Maybe I was just cooking for thirty because I was deliriously happy. Delirious, anyway.

About an hour before the happy couple was due to arrive, I decided to finish getting ready. I lit the candles on the dining room table so that they could burn down. You know, just a little. You don't want your candles to look like they just came out of the box. Brunch should look casually comfortable even if you've been up half the night nervously cooking and planning. I'd set the table with our good autumn china, lots of candles, and, of course, those gorgeous red and orange maple leaves. It was lovely. And gracious, damn it.

I headed upstairs to fix my hair. Now, when I am worried, which I might have been just a bit, my hair tends to become a . . . focus. Normally my head looks like a bit of an unmade bed. It is an unruly mass of stripy peanut-butter-and-jelly curls which on any normal day I embrace. I sometimes even love them. But when I am worried or upset, which I might have been, I try to—and there is no good explanation for this—I try to tame those curls.

I use foam. I use gel. I use blow-dryers. There are round brushes, and there are hair sprays. The bathroom is quickly a fog of products that would make a 1950s beauty shop blush. Somehow, I decide, certainly not consciously but it feels like a decision, that if I can just this once manage my hair, well then maybe I can get through whatever is in front of me. I mean, really, how tough can the rest of the world be if I've managed to whip this mass of hair into submission?

So on this particular day, my hair was fluffed and straightened and gelled and even curling-ironed to within an inch of its . . . and my . . . life. I was just getting my bangs into some kind of order when I noticed the smell. It was a vague sort of burning smell. I looked at that damned curling iron and, as one does, started talking to it.

"Now listen to me! Not now, mister!" Without preamble, the curling iron had developed a gender. A gender that clearly wasn't mine. But if you're going to talk to an inanimate object, you've got to call it something, and "mister!" seemed appropriate.

"Come on," I pleaded. "Just *pleasepleaseplease* finish what we have started here!" I guess it seemed like the kind of job that required a partnership, and the curling iron had always been an Old Team Spirit sort of guy before. Surely he'd listen to reason.

"Look, I need this damned wave. It's important. I mean it. Not. Right. Now!"

I might have been gesturing. Just a bit. I did not need to lose this fight on this of all mornings.

Then I realized that the burning smell might not actually be coming from the curling iron. Well, that was a relief. I might be able to get the wave to work, after all. But . . . well . . . if it wasn't the curling iron . . .?

I walked out into my bedroom and smelled that burning smell much more strongly. As I got to the hall, I finally saw the smoke. Yes, of course, the smoke. Because that's what I needed this morning. Smoke. Smoke? Oh my God! The house was on fire!

I ran to the top of the steps as the smoke was literally billowing from the vestibule up the stairs. Not one single smoke alarm was ringing. Not one. I guess I shouldn't have ignored those battery beeps. I screamed for Eli.

"Eli, wake up right now! The house is on fire! Get the animals! Hurry, honey, come on. Run!"

For the first time in fifteen years, Eli jumped out of bed. Well, that was something, at least.[6]

I screamed for John while I grabbed my inhaler. Eli and I have asthma. I imagined that this smoke was going to be trouble for at least the two of us. Well, also, we'd be homeless and possibly burned, but the asthma was kind of the immediate issue.

"John!" It might have been a screech, but let's call it a scream. An entirely appropriate scream. After all, our house was burning down around us and I'd seen those '70s disaster films. Screaming is totally the right thing to do.

Turns out, my husband was in the library. Downstairs. The library downstairs that is directly adjacent to the vestibule. That would be the vestibule with all the billowing smoke. Billowing. Really.

Mr. Calm was reading. Quietly steadying himself before the ski . . . er . . . aficionado . . . bum . . . whatever . . . arrived.[7]

I screamed, "John, Fire!"

He jumped up and ran into the hallway, coughing. How had he not noticed the smoke?

"It's the dining room," he quickly diagnosed.

Well, that's great. What do I care if it's the dining room?

---

6. Want to know how to get your fifteen-year-old out of bed on a Saturday morning? Set your house on fire. Works like a charm.

7. Which led me to wonder if his dick would have to be on fire before he noticed the smoke.

THE HOUSE IS ON FIRE!

Wait, the dining room? That took a second to register. The curling iron was upstairs. The oven was in the kitchen. What the hell was my curling iron doing in the dining room? Oh, right, the curling iron was upstairs. The fire was downstairs. This was not about the curling iron. Which was, for just a second, a bit of a relief. I mean, I wasn't burning my house down for the perfect wave, so at least there was that, right?

I ran for the fire extinguisher. Just as a point of interest, do *you* know how to work a fire extinguisher? No? Neither did I. And what I'm sure they never told me was that you can't read that little print on the side of the extinguisher when everything all around you is billowing smoke, either.

Shit.

Then that little phrase "the dining room" hit me again. The dining room? What's in the dining room? Oh, God, the leaves.

And the candles.

Well, shitshitshit.

John had, after breaking away from his book, found a bucket of water and a pile of towels. He doused the table, the candles, and those very decorative maple leaves before we were finally burned out of house and home by the best of intentions. Smoke and steam filled the house, but eventually there was no more fire. The table hissed and sputtered as Eli ran to turn on the attic fan. We opened the doors and the windows. When the air began to clear we could see that the ceilings were now a very stylish black. The dining room table, an eight-foot-long oak slab, was smoldering. Apparently, when the leaves had caught fire they burned a deep, wide black gash in the table. Not lovely. Nor gracious.

Brunch was in about an hour, and my hair was decidedly worse than when I'd begun.

Well, shit.[8]

By the time Jett and Hannah arrived, our pal Rick was sanding the sooty gash in the table. He'd come over on short notice and was busy saving us, yet again. You might think that it was just a brunch, so we could easily just move somewhere else. The kitchen, for example. Or perhaps the clearly untouched library. But I might not have mentioned that after the brunch—this oh-so-light-and-cheery brunch—we were hosting a dinner party. Because, really, who wouldn't?

So, while there was nothing I could do about the ceilings before our friends Jack, Karen, Bob, and Anette arrived, I could at least get some of the soot sanded off the table and all those ashes vacuumed. That seemed doable. Because, you know, in general you really do not want ashes all over the sideboard at a dinner party. I'd cover it with a cloth, and we'd all just do the best we could.

I was guessing that the dinner conversation would be pretty well limited. "So, Ellen, what did you do today?"

"Set the house on fire and fed brunch to a ski bum. How about you?"

Good grief.

One awkward meal at a time.

ooooo

Brunch with Jett was the longest three hours any of us had probably ever spent. It was . . . uncomfortable. At one point, he followed Hannah into the bathroom and closed the door. We're not, traditionally, a family that keeps guns, but I swear if we had been that family, this

---

8. My mother used to say "shit" when she was dismayed. I used to be young and cool and hip and I tossed around the word "fuck" with abandon. Now I find myself saying "shit." Is this an age thing or more of a turning-into-your-mother thing? Neither thought is a particularly gratifying one.

would have been the point in the story where we had to explain to the officer about the frightful accidental discharge.

"Honest, Officer. I can't imagine how it happened. One minute we were chatting about . . . well, hell, I have no idea, but I know I didn't mean to shoot him. Honest."

John, in his careful way, later speculated that Jett was possibly the single most boring guest who had ever been to our house . . . bless his heart.[9] To be fair, John was probably nervous. Maybe a little overwhelmed. Although you would think that would be mitigated some as we've matured. No matter. The flow of wit and mirth was a bit blocked. Hannah, to her everlasting credit, looked worried every time her beau opened his mouth. To everyone's relief, he did that less and less as the morning wore on.

But, Jett was still our guest. Brunch includes conversation. So, I tried. Well, mostly I tried. I thought, okay, so he doesn't agree with me politically, but I have a lot of friends who disagree with me. I could draw him out a bit. So I asked, "What drew you to McCain?"

"Taxes."

Okay. So this is going to take a while if we do it one word at a time, but okay, I'll bite.

"Ah. His tax policy?"

At eight bucks an hour, I wasn't sure how the McCain tax policy would affect our buddy, but I figured maybe there were other areas he'd be more chatty about. So I pushed on.

"What do you think of Governor Palin?"

Palin had been a polarizing choice and had not yet really impressed a lot of folks. I figured this would give him a stage.

---

9. In the South and parts of the Midwest, you can insult anyone pretty much with impunity so long as you add "bless her [or in this case his] heart." Like this: "Did you see Margie at church today? My God her butt has gotten as big as a barn . . . bless her heart."

"Well, she's a governor. So she must be smarter than the media is acting like she is."

Okay. So there's that. Two sentences together was progress. I looked for common ground.

"I like her glasses."

What? I'd nearly burned my house down. Don't criticize.

Eventually they left. We, the gracious hosts, grabbed for the Motrin bottle and decided that the best strategy was to just take a nap. Everything is better after a nap, right? When we woke up, it was practically time for the dinner party. This was the day that would not end.

ooooo

At dinner, after discussion of the brunch and the house fire, talk turned to how much one could reasonably interfere in the romantic lives of adult children.

Jack and Karen thought that, really, this was off-limits.

"Look, Ellen. These kids . . . our kids . . . are adults, after all. Hell, they are the adults we raised." He had a point, sure. And added that "We raised them to be smart, thoughtful people with good values. That means it's time to watch them think for themselves. Sure, they will make a few mistakes along the way. But that's how you learn to make better decisions and better lives."

It was good, liberal parenting, well explained.

But then I chimed in. As you might imagine.

"You know, 'parenting' is a verb. It doesn't end on some magical birthday." I warmed to the topic, and John, to his credit, didn't give me the long-suffering look of someone who'd heard this a dozen times. "It's always our responsibility to set an example. To offer our thoughts. There are still lots of things to be taught. Making good marriages, and then parenting, and even as in-laws and grand-parents, we are still teaching, if only by example." I had another sip of wine.

"It's even our responsibility to show them how to handle ill-ness, and eventually to handle death. We're in this for the long haul. Our kids aren't our friends. These relationships are much deeper than that."

John was largely quiet throughout. Finally, our friends turned to him to see what he would add.

"If she marries this guy, I just may have to kill myself."

Well, I guess that summed it up.

Bob and Anette were quietly moderate. Their son, too, was in a long relationship that they did not . . . appreciate. Their son, Dan, had been dating a woman for six years now. A woman who, while in no way horrible, they thought was an especially poor match. We joked about fixing him up with Hannah. Like you do.

I met Dan for the first time in New York City, a few weeks later. He was six feet six inches tall, handsome and polite. He leaned in to conversations and offered soft, ironic commentary. He spoke eloquently and with keen intelligence. This guy was funny, tall, sweet, and liberal. He was perfect for Hannah!

I decided right then that, when it comes down to it, I do believe in arranged marriages. After all, we knew his parents. They were smart people with broad interests and good values. This could really work. I mean, sure, she should meet him at some point. And it should probably seem to be . . . well, okay, it should *be* her idea. But, c'mon. He was perfect for her.

"You know, Dan. I have a beautiful, tall, very smart daughter that I'm going to introduce you to."

He charmingly explained that he was in a relationship.

So, charming *and* loyal, too. Undeterred, I persevered.

"Is it serious?" Well, I figured that I should ask. And plant the seed.

Dipping his head shyly, he said, "Yes, it's serious."

"So how long have you been dating?" I asked.

"Six years."

"Six years? Oh, well then." I gave him my biggest smile. "That's not so serious, kiddo. If it was serious, you'd have married her by now." I'm a salesperson. Don't give me an opportunity like that if you don't want me to follow through.

"Look," I said, "when that relationship ends, call me. I think you and Hannah will really like one another."

If he was shocked, he didn't show it. He took my card and laughed in a way that may have said, "Lady, you sure are nuts, but you are a guest in my parents' home so I will humor you."

And then Bob called.

Okay, really it was a couple of months later that Bob called, but it seemed like right away. He and I had been talking about getting our kids together since the house fire.

"Ellen, guess what? We are coming up to Vermont for Christmas vacation!!"

Bob is not normally a double-exclamation-point kind of guy. He's more a full-stop sort of man. Perhaps with an occasional ellipsis. But that day, he was practically giddy. It was a double-exclamation kind of conversation. Now, Bob and Anette lived in Manhattan, but they usually came to Vermont for Christmas. So I didn't get what the big deal was.

"The boys are coming, too," he explained. "Dan and Will. And Dan's not bringing his girlfriend!!"

Aha. That was the sound of the other shoe dropping. I got it.

"Bob, we'll have a party. Let's make it something casual. How about a before-Christmas pizza party or something? No holiday foods. No dressing up. 'Casual' will be the word of the day."

Truth be told, I might have been muttering under my breath *Ohmygod ohmygod!*

I added out loud that "This is so perfect. Hannah just dumped the bum!"

And she had.

You see, she had gone to visit him in Vail for Thanksgiving vacation. I guess that everybody in this family tests out life choices on vacation. At least she hadn't tried to buy the Ski Shop or something. Anyway, Jett didn't have a car to pick her up at the airport. Neither did he, apparently, bother to borrow one. And Denver, God bless it, had the coldest November in recorded history. I'd never felt so much love for Denver. So once she'd landed, Hannah had to wait for the shuttle. On the sidewalk. In minus-seven-degree weather. God bless Denver!

She called me from the sidewalk. She wasn't happy. But then she told me all about Jett's really hard life. Again.

"Hannah, all of our lives are the sum of our choices. Jett picked hard in exchange for skiing one hundred and ten days a year. That might be the right bargain for him. It's not for me, but maybe for him." I could be generous. Well, okay, I could seem generous.

On Thanksgiving Day, he worked. And he didn't pick Hannah up in time to shop for the ingredients for her favorite holiday foods. So it was a tough holiday for her. We skyped with her as we were baking bread and roasting the turkey. Skype might be the way of the future, but it isn't the same as gathering around the stove to the smell of baking bread and roasting bird. We did our "thankfuls" over the phone.[10] I missed her like mad and could hardly keep from crying. I guessed this was what it was like to have an adult daughter. I'm not sure that I approved.

At any rate, when her Denver visit was over and it was time to fly back, good old Jett put her right back on that same shuttle. Okay, now I was starting to love him, too. Come on, Jett! Keep it up just a little longer.

And then that shuttle broke down on the way to the airport! Coldest winter on record. God, I loved Denver.

She broke up with him as soon as the plane landed.

And now, Dan Lewis was coming for pizza. Predictably,[11] they couldn't stop talking all night. Dan moved to an ottoman near where she sat on the sofa, and he did that leaning-in thing I had noticed before.

What a charmer.

Hannah giggled and glittered and tossed her hair. At the hair toss, I knew she liked him. Three days later, he invited her to go out with a group. Only, there was a giant snowstorm, so they were snowed in at our place, which meant that they had to spend the night. The weather that year was cooperating more than I could have ever hoped.

Dan broke up with his girlfriend on New Year's Eve, which was a little sad, sure, for someone. Probably. But Hannah and Dan have been a happy couple ever since. Arranged marriages. In these I now believe.[12]

---

10. Every year, we go around the dinner table and list all the things that we are thankful for. Some are small and some are big. That year, I was quietly thankful for a cold Denver. I was really rooting for Denver.

11. At least for me.

12. Well, they're not actually married . . . *yet*.

At least when I'm doing the arranging.

What I learned from all of this is the very reasonable truism that when you don't like the person your adult child is dating, you should just set your house on fire. That will surely get everyone's attention focused on the problem. You should, perhaps, read the fine print first, because fire extinguishers aren't as intuitive as you might think.

Also, use a knife and fork any old way that you like.

THE TABLE

Kyle, our carpenter/handyman friend, came a few weeks later and fixed everything. He laughed when we explained about the fire, and then he got down to business. He finished sanding what Rick had begun the day of the emergency. He evened out the big dents where fire had gouged the old oak. He worked carefully, almost lovingly, removing all of the soot. He sanded it smooth again. Next he began adding stain. In no time, the gorgeous old oak was restored to its former glory. When he added a little polyurethane to the stain, there was a quiet, happy shine.

That long oak farm table is our "fancy food" spot. It is where we have holiday meals and do most of our entertaining. This table replaced the wobbly five-legged oak table we used when the kids were little. That table, that gorgeous piece of our history, still has lots of old scars. If you look closely, there are still teensy bits of silver and red glitter deeply embedded in the grain from snowy days spent crafting homemade Valentines.

We loved that old table well. It was the spot where our kids learned about basil and garlic and where they formed their first opinions about capital punishment and the impeachment of Bill Clinton. I can see exactly where we were all sitting when we tried to explain about how an office romance was threatening to bring down a presidency.

We ate vast quantities of bacon and eggs Italian-style (with pancetta and fettuccine) at that table, and we cleaned bushels and bushels of corn there. Now that table sits in our attic, holding Christmas decorations and waiting for its next incarnation in one of the kids' homes. Homes where other children, theirs, will work on pictures of rainbows and think about climate change or the global economy. Or possibly Batman.

And meanwhile, we will all get together around the new farm table and celebrate the first flush of the garden in spring. We will lick our lips over July tomatoes and fill vases with bright mountain flowers.

We can solve problems at this table. It is the place where interesting conversation and ideas will bloom. Hopefully, we will toast some engagements and the next generation of children will gouge it with scissors and love soon.

Naked

W<small>E ARE PROBABLY NOT YOUR TYPICAL FAMILY. I</small>T'S <small>NOT LIKE</small> we're radically odd or anything. I mean, it seems to me that every family—yours too, maybe—is strange in its own way. That notion of the '50s nuclear family just doesn't fit many of us anymore. It probably never did.

So when I say that I came home and found my former husband hiding behind a cherry tree as naked as the day he was born, yelling about bears, I just want you to understand it was all perfectly reasonable.

For this family.

Mostly, anyway . . . Let me explain.

ooooo

We are going to have to back up a bit. But, you know, it's a story that ends with a naked ex-husband outside hollering about bears . . . so, it's worth it.

This all started October 24, 1987, on a sunny Saturday afternoon in St. Louis, which is the home of the beloved baseball Cardinals. It was the sixth game of the World Series and the Cards were playing the Minnesota Twins. The thing is that St. Louis is a baseball town. You don't have to be a fan of the sport . . . of any sport, actually . . . to know when the Cards are doing well; it's a citywide phenomenon. And when the team makes the Series? Well, then it's a full-on celebration. Every bar is full. Every restaurant has the game on. There are televisions in department stores and pharmacies and nail salons all glued to the game. It's a big deal. So, though I'm no kind of statistician, I can tell you that when I wandered into a bar, it was three o'clock in the afternoon and the first pitch was being thrown.

I had been separated from my former husband, Steve Stimson, for about two years by then. Steve and I still saw each other all the time. In fact, he usually came over to spend time with our two-and-a-half-year-old on Saturday afternoons. Father and son also played together in the evenings while I cooked supper, but Saturdays were when we tried solo-Steve visits.

Benjamin was a wild child. He looked a little like he was being raised by wolves rather than actual people most of the time. And Steve, like a lot of people, probably, had a hard time keeping up with that level of energy. So Saturday afternoons were about his speed. He could spend time with his kid without being too overwhelmed. He'd spend the day with us and then head back to his house for the evening . . . and probably a stiff drink.

I took this particular Saturday afternoon for a late lunch and a little baseball, while Steve chased our boy. On most weekends, I'd come home after three or four hours to find them both fast asleep on the floor under tent blankets surrounded by practically everything I owned. So I knew I had a little time to enjoy the game and the outing. A Steve-Benjamin visit was chaotic and a mess, but they both always seemed to survive.

When I walked into my favorite local restaurant/bar, Stagger Inn,[1] I saw this strikingly handsome man with curly brown hair and a gorgeous smile. I hadn't dated since Steve and I separated. I honestly didn't know if I *would* date. I didn't want a succession of friendly "uncles" in my child's life, but in my early twenties, I also didn't want to spend the rest of my days without a mate. It was a puzzle I had not begun to solve.

---

1. Yes. Stagger Inn. And, possibly, stagger out.

Oh, there was unquestionably a divorce coming. Don't get me wrong. Steve and I couldn't be in the same room for more than about fifteen minutes before we fought like rats trapped inside a coffee can. At the same time, we hadn't figured out how to get divorced yet, either. It was on the agenda, surely. But we just hadn't gotten around to it yet.

And there was this cute guy watching baseball.

Well, I figured maybe I could see if I remembered how to flirt, anyway. Flirting is a useful skill. I figured a little flirting couldn't hurt. The guy seemed to know lots of folks around the bar. Hmm. Well, so did I. It was my local too, after all. Benjamin and I had cheeseburgers and root beers here most every Friday night. I looked around the room and spotted a friend. I walked over and asked him to introduce me to that guy.

By now it was the fourth inning, and the Cards were up by two runs. And after an introduction, surprisingly,[2] we started watching the game together. We chatted a bit between action on the screen, and it turned out that he knew me.

Or, at least, *of* me. Which is sort of the same thing. Kind of, anyway.

As it turns out, we had gone to high school together. See, I was a little . . . loud . . . in high school. Okay, in life. But certainly in high school. And I was in every high school play,[3] so people often knew who I was.

Hmm. So, he knew me from Granite City High. I looked him over and figured him for an athlete. I asked if he had been on the little soccer team.

This might seem strange to people. Why not the basketball

---

2. To us, anyway.

3. And every other sort of drama going on at the time as well.

team? The football team? But this was Granite City High. Our soccer team had been state champions six years running, so "little" was actually a point of irony.

"Yeah, actually. I played all four years," he said and, perhaps unsurprisingly, went back to watching the game.

By the fifth inning, we had struck up a rhythm. A little chatting back and forth around and between the game. It was really nice. So, I would say something, and then he'd quietly reply and I'd burst out laughing. I'm not a quiet laugher. But, hey, this guy was funny. I desperately needed funny in my life at the time. And he seemed to like that I laughed.

In the sixth inning, the Twins were up by five runs. So we gave up on the game and gave into the conversation by heading over to a table. We talked nonstop for three hours. This guy had a soft voice and an easy laugh. He ducked his head when he talked. I loved that. When he was thoughtful he bit his lip. This was way before Bill Clinton adopted that lip-bite, and it was compelling on the face of this gentle, funny guy. And he looked right at me when I talked, with these completely exquisite blue eyes. At the end of that afternoon, he walked me outside and kissed my cheek.

I must have said something like, "Look, I have a baby, so I really can't invite you back to my place."[4]

And he explained that he wasn't that kind of guy. Still, I gave him my number and went home feeling that special kind of hopeful. Buoyant, even. That feeling you have when your heart recognizes one of its own kind.

Only then . . . he didn't call.

Of course, Sunday would have been too soon. I knew that.

---

4. Wait till he sees what kind of baby. Over two, and monster-sized. But, you know, my baby.

He didn't want to seem overeager. I get that. Monday might have worked, though. Eager, but not too eager. Surely Tuesday. Nope, not Tuesday.

The week wore on, and I decided, in that grandiose certainty of a twenty-something, that I would spend my life single . . . focused on Benjamin. Besides, we didn't need a man to round things out. No, we didn't. Benjamin and I were doing just fine on our own.

Well, that was Wednesday anyway.

By Thursday I was looking him up in the phone book and thinking about calling.

On Friday, I realized that all this anxiety was a folly. I needed to finalize this divorce from Steve and move on with my single life. I was still married. Sort of married, anyway. And so, divorce. Divorce was key. And besides, men were a nice accessory, but surely they weren't necessary.[5]

Anyway, when I drove by Stagger Inn on Saturday, they had just hung the sign advertising the annual Halloween party. By noon I had a plan, and by two I had a costume. I act quickly when I have a good idea. When I have a bad idea, too, if we're being honest, but this seemed like a good idea. So anyway, I figured that on Saturday I would wear a witchy hat and cape in black and purple to take Benjamin trick-or-treating. It was a nice, motherly Halloween costume. Then I would race over to my sister's house, where Benjamin would spend the night so that I could go out and . . . well . . . track down[6] . . . the cute guy who'd had my number for a week and never once picked up the phone. You know, like you would do in a similar situation. Wouldn't you?

---

5. I don't know, like a nice purse, I guess. Though, to be fair, a nice purse *is* a nice purse.

6. Not stalk. Definitely not stalk.

After loading my son up with candy and smiles, I drove over to my sister's place and changed into a black leotard and black tights. I made a tail out of some old stockings, and I drew whiskers on my face. My mom had made me a headband with little black felt cat ears on it years before. So I put that to use. I was going to be a hot Halloween kitty.

Cute Guy wouldn't know what hit him.

Only, as it turns out, I went to the party with my erstwhile husband. Well, I didn't exactly mean to . . . exactly. It just sort of . . . happened. As many things seem to in my life.

First, of course, Steve wanted to come along when I took Benjamin trick-or-treating. That went well enough. But then he came over to my place to get his safari jacket. Apparently Steve had decided that he was going out for the rest of the evening as Bwana, the Great Hunter,[7] while I was transforming into Super Kitty, so he needed the jacket. Anyway, one thing led to the inevitable other, and somehow it happened that my sister was coming to the party, too. Then Steve's sister, Mindy, was coming as well. So my sister-in-law was joining me. And my soon-to-be-ex-husband. And our boy. And my soon-to-be-I-hoped-new-boyfriend. It was a fucking Alan Alda movie. Cheska was right. But you know, I was a responsible adult. Sort of. So I argued that someone had to stay with Benjamin. I wasn't taking him to Stagger Inn for the Halloween party. He was two and a half, after all. Cheeseburgers and root beer in the afternoon, sure. A raucous Halloween party, no. After a bit of thought, my sister suggested hot cocoa to Benjamin and so it turned into just Steve and Mindy and me. Not perfect, but really, what is?

Steve and I couldn't be married, but we were sort of beginning

---

7. One of the many examples of our incompatibilities.

to figure out how to be related. We had a child, who needed us. There were many years of raising that child to come. We didn't like each other much after having a wildly unhappy few months as a married couple, but this life of ours was going to be long. And apparently Steve was coming along for the whole ride with Benjamin and me.

We had to figure it out.

Perhaps we could go to the same party without going . . . together. Sort of like going with your older brother to a dance. Your older brother and his sister. Who in this scenario would be your sister, I guess. You go awkwardly, but at least everybody gets to go. Family was always a complicated concept for me.

Once we had worked out the arrangement and I had kissed my boy good night, we headed to the party. I walked into Stagger Inn and spotted Cute Guy immediately. He had on heavy cowboy boots, a flannel shirt, a floppy hillbilly sort of hat, and a long goofy beard. He was talking in a big group of people. People that I knew. I sidled up and joined the conversation. I was looking for my chance, and it came faster than I would have imagined.

My friend Bob had just bought a round, and was passing them out. He asked if I knew John.

"John?" I asked with great clarity and not a little volume.

"Yeah, John Rushing." He may have gestured at the faux-billy.

"Do. I. Know. John?" I asked, getting the attention of pretty well the whole group. John, formerly Cute Guy,[8] seemed to be smiling uneasily behind his mountain-man costume beard.

"As a matter of fact, Bob, I *do* know John. We met last weekend. I gave him my . . . Phone. Number." I might have been enunci-

---

8. Well, he was still cute, of course, but I figure I should give him a real name at this stage.

ating a little bit sharply at the time. That sort of thing happens when you haven't been called in a week.

"And do you know what?"

No one did.

"He didn't *use* it."

The chorus of "Ohhhhhhhh!" and "John? What? Ohhhhhh!" rang out in a big, group, dramatic commentary.

It was quite satisfying.[9]

Everyone got a big laugh out of it, and he made his way around the circle to me.

John started in sort of sheepishly. "I was going to call. I swear. It was just a weird week."

I was smiling boldly now. It felt good to gain a bit of the side of the right, here. Then I noticed the bartender calling me over. I had a phone call.

Oh dear.

It was, of course, my sister. Benjamin had slammed his finger in a drawer and needed his mommy. So I hung up the phone, excused myself, and found Steve and Mindy in the other room. We left together. Wonder what Cute Guy thought of that?

I found out the next day. And the day after that. Because, again, the phone didn't ring.

By Tuesday I had just about given up. On John. On men in general. On using the phone for anything. It wasn't pretty. But I still needed to feed this monster baby, so sitting by the phone waiting on a guy to call who was steadily becoming less cute in my memory, wasn't solving anything. I bundled my boy into the car with a handful of his toys and a bottle of bubbles. We headed to National for groceries.

---

9. I guess I hadn't left the dramatic gestures behind in high school.

We had just finished shopping and were headed to the check-out, with Benjamin blowing bubbles at passersby, when I looked over and saw our Mr. Rushing (Cute Guy) in the checkout lane ahead of us.

Well, I couldn't resist, could I?

I sang out, "So, do you really eat white bread?"

Poor guy, he couldn't even shop in this town without running into me. And I was being . . . well, a bit pointed in my questions. As I can sometimes be. But only when provoked.

He got flustered. I know this because he left his wallet at the register. The cashier called out to stop him from leaving. "Sir! Your wallet! Sir!"

He made a face. It was really the cutest face, ever. I had to give him credit for that, anyway.

"I . . . I was going to call tonight," he offered. "Is that still all right?"

I might have arched an eyebrow. Possibly.

"It might be all right. Why don't you try dialing and we'll both find out?"

I paid and headed out with a cart full of groceries and giant-child, wondering if this guy's finger would ever work. Er . . . you know, if he would call.

Turns out it did. He did.

The phone was ringing when we got home. I hadn't carried in all the groceries when I answered, but I grabbed some wooden spoons off the counter and a couple of pans. I sat Benjamin down in front of them and had him make a kitchen band, while I sat in the corner twirling the phone cord to begin a conversation that has, so far, lasted twenty-five years.

In December, I told Steve.

"Is this that guy from Halloween?" he asked.

I responded in what seemed like one breath. "Yes. Look, I'm in love. I'm thinking about the rest of my life, which should probably include a divorce. I'm going to introduce John to Benjamin soon and see how they fit." Best to just get that all out, right?

"Well, what does this guy do for a living?" Suddenly Steve was Father of the Bride. Ex-Husband of the Bride? If there was a game show for weirdest conversations, this one would have been in the running.

After a few minutes of back and forth, Steve said in a much more serious tone, "Look, after a while. Not right away, but after a while. I want to see the two of them together, too. For me."

Seemed reasonable.

First my child. Then my ex. Let's see what you're made of, Cute Guy.

ooooo

December seemed like a good time to get my son and my new love together. John and I planned a Christmas-tree outing. He needed a tree, and Benjamin always needed space. I figured a gigantic Christmas-tree forest might be just big enough.

Benjamin and I drove over to John's apartment to pick him up. We climbed out of the car and John immediately took my boy by the hand and said, "Hey, kid. Come in here and let me show you something."

I might have panicked.

He was taking my son into his kitchen? And he called him "kid." Couldn't he see that this was a baby? This guy was just twenty-four, I guess. He didn't really know anything, right? What did I expect? My heart raced.

Shit.

What if he's a pedophile, and this was the beginning of his cultivation? What had I been thinking? Who was this guy? I mean, sure, he was cute. But what, after all, did I really know about him?[10]

I tiptoed over to the kitchen door so I could see exactly what was going on.

John told Benjamin to close his eyes and open his mouth. Then, with great fanfare, he squirted canned whipped cream straight into the little guy's mouth. And a little dollop on his chin for good measure.

There was giggling.

I got a squirt of my own.

As beginnings go, it was a good one.

We left for the tree farm in a cloud of cream and giggles.

ooooo

A couple of weeks later, I left Benjamin with Steve for a visit with the Stimson family. Steve's sister is Benjamin's much-adored Aunt Mindy. Aunt Mindy and Steve's parents, of course, doted on Benjamin, and as the only grandchild he sort of stole the show.

John and I spent the day in downtown St. Louis. It was a lovely way to spend the holiday with a new crush that was clearly showing all the signs of being young love. We had a glass of champagne at the Broadway Oyster Bar and toasted "whatever comes next." We had no idea what we had signed up for, of course, but we were young and up for whatever was in front of us.

Snow began to fall in tiny snowflakes as we walked from shop to shop. It felt like a blessing. We found an ornament for John's tree that seemed just right. It was a sax-playing Santa they called St. Louie Nick, and it was just the right level of hip and just the right level of traditional.[11]

---

10. Overreact? Me? Perish the thought.

11. It's still on the family tree.

Christmas was important to us, and the next year with Benjamin this turned into an annual tradition. We called it Christmas Adventure. It has been a feature in every December of our lives since. We go somewhere cool (first this was to St. Louis and later, to other places), have a big holiday dinner, stay overnight in a hotel, and eat a meandering festive brunch the next day. Everyone gets to choose a special new ornament for the tree,[12] and in this way we kick off the annual December celebration of love.

By the first day of preschool, Benjamin introduced us all to his new teacher.

"This is Mommy. And this is my dad. And this is my other dad."

Steve came to the wedding. Under the Christmas tree, of course.

○○○○○

So that's the backstory. It sounds very sweet, and it was. There were a lot of years where things weren't smooth. We didn't become a big happy family right away. It took a while to get here. But get here we did. Eventually.

Now, the few other bits you should know. One thing that kind of comes up again and again is that we are sort of a naked family. Not a nudist family or anything.

We are not weird.

Just naked. Occasionally.

When the kids were little, they ran around the yard naked, playing in the water hose all summer long. Hannah, our daughter, was naked more than she was dressed for much of her toddlerhood.

"Nakey! I wanna be nakey!" rang out till she was about five. Now, that might seem a bit embarrassing to an adult, but truth be

---

12. As the family has gotten larger, everyone still gets a new ornament. This makes for a pretty crowded but happy tree.

told, at twenty-something, excepting a few more curves, Hannah in her bikini really doesn't seem all that different to me. She might as well be a naked five-year-old running through the water hose.

We are, also, the kind of people that traipse out of the bathtub toweling our hair and leaving wet footprints en route to the bedrooms. This is, perhaps, compounded by the geography of our Vermont house.

See, the bedrooms in our house are on the second floor. And the good bathroom is downstairs, near the guest room. Well, yeah, there are two bathrooms upstairs. But one is only a half bath so it only half counts.[13] And the master bathroom is, for a lot of reasons, just not up to the job. It's a nice bathroom, of course. John showers there. I brush my teeth there. But it's just not right for bathing. The tub is wrong. It's too big. Takes forever to fill. You'll have to trust me. I am a bath expert and that tub, while very charming in its own way, does not work for me.

But the first-floor bathroom. Well, that's different. It's great. The bathtub has a single Jacuzzi, which we had installed. I love the way the tub is shaped. It's perfect for soaking and for reading, which is an essential bathtime activity as far as I'm concerned. Plus it has a really powerful showerhead. Stand under it too long and it would leave marks on you. It's a shower like a shower oughta be. Not like that piddly shower upstairs. This is a shower that could strip paint.

So, the family divides by bathing type. John uses the master. Eli and I use the first floor. And the older kids make do when they are here. Of course, between the first-floor bath and the second-floor bedrooms there is a little naked traipsing. Maybe a little more than is, strictly speaking, necessary.

---

13. It used to be a full bath, but then we expanded Eli's bedroom when it seemed like maybe the other kids were never gonna actually move out. Only then they did. Right after the renovation. Oh well. That tub was also no good in its own way too.

We have robes, of course. Eli is not so much into naked as a public experience. So he has a fluffy red robe. I, too, have a robe. Unfortunately, it's never in the room that I need it to be. I mean, planning hasn't always been my strongest skill. So the robe is usually somewhere that I'm not. Which leads to a few naked rules. My kids thought every family had naked rules. We had a surprised conversation about this three times with young teenagers.

"Ohmygod did you know some people have never seen their parents naked?!"

Or:

"Guess what? The [Fill in the blank best friend's family] are completely repressed. They are never naked. Never. I don't know how they get dressed. They probably even shower in the dark."

Or the astute:

"Umm, I think maybe you guys are weird."

Anyway, I announce my presence when there's going to be Naked Mom walking around the house. I call out, and if there are any visitors with the kids, I give them fair warning.

"Hey! Is anybody here besides us?" I'll call.

Sometimes I can hear laughing boys headed in my direction when I'm at the computer . . . alternatively clad. Well, you know, I'm dripping my way along the hallway and I stop—just for a second, I mean, really fast—to check my email. And sometimes I forget. Or I get caught up in something. And . . . anyway, so I'm there at the computer. Naked. And I hear the kids coming, so I'll yell out, "WAIT! I'm not dressed!"

That sort of thing.

It's a system. It works. Mostly.

There are inevitably (rarely, I swear), hardly ever, really, days when it doesn't.

ooooo

Benjamin was at our home alone when he got a phone call from an old high school girlfriend. This had been the love of his young life, and they had been emailing recently. They were doing that little dance that we all have done with old flames at one time or another. Anyway, it turns out that she was flying to the East Coast from St. Louis, and would have an overnight just a couple of hours from our house. So, of course, he had to go. I mean, normally she lived a thousand miles away. It didn't seem like there was any question at all that he'd drive two hours to see her.

He had the house to himself on the day of her visit, and apparently he ran around the whole place getting ready. He showered. He tried on different outfits. In a totally confident and manly way, of course. But it was important to find the right outfit. You understand. He lays out his clothes on his bed, and then remembers that his sister has a full-length mirror in her room. So he runs in there to take a look at himself.

Naked.

Now, why he needed to see himself naked in a full-length mirror before driving two hours to see an old girlfriend, I don't know. I didn't need to know then. I don't need to know now. Believe me, I never asked. But apparently, he did need to do this. It was important.

So, he inspects . . . the view, I guess. And he decides that everything meets with his approval. Then he heads back to his bedroom.

At least that was the plan.

See, we live in an old farmhouse. And that farmhouse has these beautiful, if ancient, glass doorknobs. And those doorknobs sometimes . . . fall off. You reach for the doorknob thinking that you'll just fling open a door, and the knob comes off in your hand. So we have pliers or someone on the other side of our doors to get them working again, until Kyle, the handyman, can come reattach the knob. That gives us a few more months out of them.

We've done this for years. Well, they're very nice doorknobs.

But, see, here's the thing. Benjamin was on the inside of his sister's bedroom, locked in. Alone in the house. With no doorknob. Okay, so he had the doorknob, but it wasn't helping very much since it wasn't attached to the door.

Hmm.

So a screwdriver or pliers would help. But, as it turns out, he didn't bring one of those into the bedroom when he dashed in there naked. So that was no good. He tried to make do.

He folded up a clothes hanger and gave that a try. Surprisingly, no luck. The clock was ticking. He looked around the room and spotted, of all things, his sister's high heel shoe. Well, it *is* pointy. Sort of like a screwdriver. If you look at it from the right[14] perspective.

No good. And terrible for the shoe.

He started rummaging through Hannah's drawers. There had to be some help around there somewhere. But nothing.

He looked up at the door, then around the room. He figured that these were desperate times and tried the window. Sure enough, the window would open. But he wasn't exactly . . . well, he was naked.

Looking back around the room, his eye latched on to a pair of pink boy shorts in Hannah's drawer. They were tight on her long, very slender frame. Benjamin is six four. But he imagined that being completely naked on the roof of your parents' house just wasn't done, I guess.

He tugged on the boy shorts[15] and hustled out onto the roof. Barefoot, he scrambled down to the edge of the roof and wondered, briefly, if the gardening neighbors up the hill were working in their yard today. Well, not much to do about it now.

---

14. Desperate.

15. I guess they do have "boy" in the name. Next time I'm going to introduce him to a "boy towel" or a "boy raincoat."

In that calculation that young men must make all the time, Benjamin looked at himself, the edge of the roof, and the distance to the ground. He's always been athletic. And there was a girl waiting for him. She was certainly hoping he was wearing the outfit he'd planned rather than a pair of his sister's underwear. Doing the math he . . . well, you know what he did.

He jumped.

Naturally, he sprained his ankle.

Limping back into the house, he quickly changed from his transvestite-at-the-end-of-the-dance look into something more appropriate, iced his already-swelling ankle, and drove away quickly. Because, after his little roof-jumping incident, he was already late to meet the plane. It took about five miles for the flashing lights to catch his attention.

Half an hour later he was on his way, with a speeding ticket and a throbbing ankle.

This could have happened to anyone, of course. Only mostly it's the sort of thing that seems to happen to us. A lot.

ooooo

Still, none of that really explains the Thanksgiving-naked-former-husband-bear problem, but it does sort of lay out the landscape.

Anyway, it was Thanksgiving and Steve had come to visit. Steve and I couldn't really be married all those years ago, but we had indeed figured out how to be related. He was a part of my family now in an ongoing way. There were whole years when I couldn't stand to be in the same room with Steve, but I did want him to be a part of his son's life. Hell, we were even still connected by a name.

You'll note that Steve is a Stimson, and so am I. When we married I was very young, and my politics weren't quite where they were going to end up. And so I took Steve's last name. Then we had Benjamin. Then we got divorced. You'd imagine that that would be where

I changed my name back, but at the time it was important to Benjamin that we were all connected by a last name.[16] Then, of course, I married John. But rather than taking John's name or my own, I kept Benjamin's last name (and consequently Steve's). It's all a little complicated, but the upshot is that Steve was a part of the family, with us for holidays and events and prone to all the little family . . . traits . . . that the rest of us seem to display. On his Thanksgiving trip to Vermont, John picked Steve up at the Albany airport and they both came home smelling like a tavern. This, anyway, was not typical.

Well, the Albany airport part *was* typical. A little counterintuitively, it is quicker to fly into Albany and drive to Dorset than it is to fly into the nearest Vermont airport. The part that was unusual was the aroma. John and Steve get along pretty well, but they didn't usually stop off at a bar on the way home. It was a curious situation.

"So . . . uh . . . what's with the . . . smell?" I'm sure I didn't raise an eyebrow or anything. That would have been rude.

The story staggered out.

It seems that Steve had been making and aging bourbon in his basement. He'd wanted to surprise us with a bottle; only, he had been stopped in airport security with something that sounded suspiciously like sloshing.

"Sir, do you have any liquids in that bag?"

"Aaah . . . liquids?" Steve responded, as if somehow this was a new word that had slipped by him. Liquids? Oh, you mean *liquids*.

"Yes, sir. *Liquids*," said the voice of authority.

"Like shampoo?" Steve seemed to need a bit more clarification about what qualified as a liquid. And really, don't we all?

"Well, you can have three ounces of things like shampoo, but

---

16. At about three, he'd wondered if we would still be "related" if I changed my name. And that was that. A Stimson I would stay.

do you have anything more than that?" I'm guessing that TSA wasn't satisfied that three ounces of shampoo would slosh audibly.

"Now . . . how . . . much . . . exactly . . . *is* three ounces? What size . . . container . . . might that beeeee?"

Steve stretched out these sentences with elongated words and punctuated pauses in between each and every word. And he wrinkled up his face using the international sign that indicated he had either managed to sit in something moist or he was mightily . . . perturbed.

So here is Steve, this big, burly guy. He carried a full beard for most of his life and went around in all these tweedy vests and coats and hats, which usually had lots of metal things sticking out of pockets of all sizes. There might well be a compass jutting out of a pocket just in case some emergency orienteering was needed in Albany. He always wore a big watch with lots of dials and gadgets. There was usually a pair of binoculars around his neck in case a rare piping plover flew over. I mean, really, you just never knew. Plus, he usually carried himself bigger than he was. He was a presence in a room. He looked a bit like an English gentleman from around 1890 coming out to inspect the grounds.

However, in the twenty-first-century Albany airport, the look wasn't really working for him. At least not in the way that he'd hoped.

"Sir, we'd like to search your bag."

"But I am already off your plane, son." Steve later said the fellow looked like he was about twelve years old. And, you know, he had a point. He was *leaving* the airport. *After* the flight.

"Yes, sir. But you are still in a secure area, and we'd like to search your bag."

I'm pretty sure that Steve imagined that he was being helpful when he said, "Listen, if you'll just get out of my way I will leave your secure area just as fast as I possibly can." See, he was just making this TSA guy's life simpler. Thoughtful of him, really.

That's when the rest of the TSA detail showed up. Some of them were, apparently, older than twelve. They had walkie-talkies, too, which is always a bad sign. The team reached for Steve's bag.

And, of course, Steve pulled it back from them. Because, really, he was *off* the plane already. This was silly.

The TSA guys pulled harder, because that sloshing was certainly pronounced now. And, of course, the bag wound up on the floor with bourbon gushing out . . . everywhere. It got on Steve's vest . . . the twelve-year-old security guy . . . the walkie-talkies . . . and every piece of clothing that he'd packed . . . as it went crashing down to the secure area's now very smelly tiled floor. In Albany, it was partly cloudy with a chance of bourbon that day.

Several hours passed before Steve was allowed to leave the secure area. He was rather vague about where he'd been and what all they had talked to him about. And, we never did get to taste that particular vintage.

Steve was all smiles when he told the story, though. There may have been just the slightest slur when he spoke.

ooooo

Anyway, Steve was our Thanksgiving guest. Sobered up and rested. He was using our first-floor guest room with the wonderful screened porch that overlooks the chickens and the garden, and incidentally, has its own bathroom, while he stayed with us. The first-floor bathroom. *My* bathroom.

I had come to sort of hate having guests. Even guests that I loved. Because, of course, it meant that I had to use the little drippy shower in the master bathroom upstairs. It tarnished the joy of company a bit, I can tell you.

So anyway, Steve had the good bathroom, and he was taking every advantage of it. It seemed like I heard that Jacuzzi going at all hours of the day and night. How often does one man need to bathe? I mean, yeah, Steve was a big, burly, hairy guy who smelled like the floor of a distillery when he got here, but c'mon.

The man lived in Edwardsville, Illinois, so Vermont was a bit of a ways to come. Rather than just coming in for Thanksgiving, Steve was staying the week. So maybe I was feeling a little put out. A week without *my* bathroom. But still, did he have to flaunt that he was using the good tub? I mean, really.

At any rate, I had run out to the store to get some more pecans for the baking that I was doing. I came back in, humming and happy. I love everything about Thanksgiving. We take long, woodsy walks with the dogs. Hannah and I bake John's grandmother's bread recipe. I cook everyone's favorite foods. We play games and watch movies. And with these pecans I should have everything we'd need for a great holiday meal.

I wandered into the library to turn on some Van Morrison, when I heard the Jacuzzi going . . . again! God, this man bathes a lot. Certainly more than when we were married. Well, I quickly told myself that it was just for the week, at least. I headed back into the kitchen to turn the speakers on in there. And that's when I saw "it."

Did I mention Steve's size? Six foot three, with broad shoulders and a big beard. In fact, he generally resembled a bear. Only, not right then, actually. At that moment, he was outside my kitchen window, standing behind a gangly cherry tree which covered him exactly not at all—Naked. Like, really, really, naked.[17] He was peering around (well, as much "around" as the diameter allowed) the trunk of the cherry tree toward the house.

---

17. Yes, there are degrees of Naked. And he was certainly in the Really Naked category. Which is a bit more intense than Starkers and not quite up to You're Under Arrest Naked.

I flung open the old-fashioned windows in the kitchen and yelled, "Steve! What the hell?!"

Alzheimer's. It couldn't be Alzheimer's, could it? He's too young. But what the . . . ?

"Oh, Ell-*ennnn*." He said my name in this multisyllabic whine with his face wrinkled up and his mouth open. It was almost as if I was trying to take his hidden bourbon away. Though where he was hiding it might have been a serious question.

I, I think reasonably in the circumstances, asked, "What are you doing out there?"

Steve started to explain that "Well, I was in the tub and I got this idea about filling up water balloons. I thought I'd surprise Eli when he got back with John. After that little episode last night,[18] I am planning Total Retaliation. I didn't know how long they'd be gone."

Water balloons?

Uh-huh.

I didn't get it.

"Steve," I said in that voice you, yourself, might use when confronting a naked ex-husband in your backyard . . . or a mental patient. "Steve, you are outside. Naked."

I figured someone had to be clear about this.

"There's a bear."

Uh-huh.

Did he just say "bear"? In the Jacuzzi? Did it chase him outside? Where are the dogs? Wait, there can't be a bear in the Jacuzzi. Right? It's Vermont, but c'mon.

---

18. Eli had welcomed Steve with a little christening water balloon, which had somehow turned into all-family water-balloon warfare in the library. Poor Steve had been unarmed upon arrival and had run into the house for cover, where someone had given him a little ammunition of his own. One thing inevitably led to another and before you knew it we were all throwing water balloons like five-year-olds at a birthday party.

"What?" I said. Now, as rejoinders go it wasn't particularly clever, but I figured it would open up a thread I could grab onto.

"I think there's a bear," Steve very carefully explained.

"Where?"

"By the house," he answered.

Well, I was *in* the house. I had just driven up our hill, parked in the driveway, and walked into the house. I managed all that without seeing . . . anything. No lions. No tigers. No bears. No squirrels, even. Quiet day as far as I could see.

"Steve, I just came in the house . . ."

"I. Am. Telling. You. I. Saw. A. Bear!" He was getting a little louder. Naked and now loud. But, to be honest, he did seem actually scared. And he was outside in my yard naked, which was, even for Steve, a little unusual.

Maybe there *was* a bear.

Now where did I leave my camera?

I walked over to the mudroom and looked outside. Nope. No bear. I opened the back door and walked around the house. I was standing about twenty feet from Steve, who was at this point bent over and trying to hide his . . . particulars . . . while standing behind the tiniest cherry tree in the world. It suddenly (and just now, oddly enough) struck me as really, really funny. I looked down and saw that he had a bunch of wadded-up balloons in his hand. And that was all it took.

I started laughing. And I just couldn't stop.

This, of course, got the dogs' attention. All three came running outside to see what was happening. And, as you'd expect, the dogs recognized that a large naked man hiding behind the tree was not a normal thing, so they started barking.

Steve explained to his cackling ex-wife and her barking pack that "I was just filling the tub and nobody was here and I thought about the balloons. But the balloons wouldn't fit on the faucet in the tub, and your kitchen sink was full of brining turkey. So then I thought I'd just run out here and fill them with the hose . . ." His voice trailed off as I struggled to get a breath.

Oh, of course. Water balloons. The water in the tub must have made him think of the balloons and so he just grabbed them up and . . . sure. Then he thought he saw a bear and panicked. All perfectly sensible.

I laughed harder. The dogs barked louder.

Pippi, one of our dogs, wandered over to Steve. Barked. Sniffed. Barked some more.

I couldn't talk. I could barely breathe.

You may not know this, but there are very few men in the world who—when naked—enjoy being laughed at quite that enthusiastically. And Steve had had enough. He straightened up to his full height. Naked, but proud, he mustered whatever dignity was left to him and marched . . . Marched . . . into the house. To the Jacuzzi, presumably, muttering the whole while, "I am telling you, there was a God. Damned. Bear!"

I gathered up what breath I could and the pack of dogs and went back into the kitchen. Still smiling . . . and occasionally giggling, to be truthful . . . I started rolling out the dough for our nutroll on the counter. My hands were covered in flour when I heard, "Ell-*ennnn!*"

Steve was screaming my name from the bathroom. The bear, again? Was Steve back out in the yard? I peeked out the window just in case. No. This time he was actually *in* the bathroom. Well, at least there was that. Turns out he was in the bathroom, where the doorknob had just fallen off in his hand.

I sure hoped he had a robe in there.

○○○○○

BY THE BACK DOOR

In our farmhouse kitchen tucked into a little nook, there is an old French walnut table. This table is oval, and it has four beautifully carved legs. It sits in an alcove, where we have cushy banquettes built into the walls and chairs around the other side. The banquettes are covered in a sturdy red check. There are piles of Provençal pillows in a cheery pattern of blue, red, and yellow. The walls in this room are a color Farrow & Ball calls Orangery, but which is really a dark yellow. The walls are the color of afternoon light on a sunshiny autumn day in Vermont.

This nook is our place for everyday breakfasts and suppers. Everyone sits there and watches whomever happens to be cooking. This table gets its share of tagliatelle with sage and pancetta topped with runny, softly fried eggs for saucing, served with the strongest Parmesan-Reggiano we can find. In winter, the slow-roasted pork tenderloin comes on a bed of curried cauliflower just after Chris Matthews has left us with lots to talk about.

These days, John and I mostly just have Eli at home for supper. The sweet, easygoing teenager looks and acts so much like his dad that it is almost as if I wasn't involved in the birth. We joke that he is the best roommate we have ever had. And on winter Saturday mornings, there are always piles of shoes by the radiator and heaping plates of lemony winter crepes like winter's citrus kiss for the boys who played poker all night out on the heated "summer" porch. Regular guests, like Steve, have joined us at this table for morning coffee and Van Morrison, playing from the speakers tucked into the cookbook shelves. Our closest friends eat pizza here while John tosses the dough dramatically and we serve up pie after pie with peas and mascarpone or fig and prosciutto.

This is the place where our regular lives get sorted.

When the older kids come for the weekends, it is where we all gather every morning, drinking thick coffee and dreaming up eggy casseroles and blueberry waffles by the dozen. On really blustery days, we might get out the deep fryer and make homemade doughnuts, which will take us till one or two o'clock to recover from well enough to think about the rest of the dwindling day. We wander in, one at a time, in jammies and robes and make our way to the coffeepot and the cream. We cook together and argue and laugh our way through whatever is in front of us. If our big dining room table is made for feasting and celebration, then this one is for nourishing ordinary ritual.[1]

ooooo

---

1. We do generally wear clothes here.

CHAPTER THREE

Real Vermonters

We wanted our kids to grow up in a village. We all wanted to live closer to the natural world. The idea of a community making a living closer to the land appealed to us deeply. Actually living in community is way different than looking in at it from vacation, though.

When we first looked at this old farmhouse in Dorset, I stood on the balcony and imagined myself outside in the mornings drinking coffee. It was a nice view of the mountain, and a great mental image for me. In my daydream, I was wearing my long, gauzy white nightgown. And I was picking flowers for the porch. I could never have done that in our old life in St. Louis.

See, there is this thing about living closely in a real community. It seems to me that there is a sort of Law of the Conservation of Privacy. Privacy is pretty straightforward, right? I can do things in private that no one knows about. If I eat peanut butter out of the jar while standing in front of the refrigerator, it's nobody's business. It's private.

That's life in a village. Your neighbors are miles away. In winter, they might as well be on the moon. So if I want to stand on the balcony in a gauzy nightgown, it's pretty much private.

Anonymity is different. If I do something anonymously, everyone can see it, but no one can connect it to me. Well, they can see it's me but it doesn't matter because they don't know who I am.

That's what city life offers. You are surrounded by a lot more people. And those people are a lot closer to you. But you are anonymous.

61

In a city, where the houses are built very close together, there is no privacy for romantic nightgowns in the yard.[1] You live near enough to others that you can't be invisible. But, interestingly enough, because so many people live so close to one another, you develop the talent for letting people remain anonymous. If you don't know that person in the grocery store personally, you can just ignore whatever it is they are doing. Well, within reason. You might not want to let them rob the place or anything, but it isn't your business if they buy six frozen dinners and a bottle of gin. It's just not. And that's life in a city like St. Louis.

Vermont, however, offers loads of privacy, but it gives you a village life without anonymity.[2] St Louis had no privacy, but plenty of anonymity.

At any rate, Vermont is my home now. I love it here. I suspect I will live here for the rest of my life. I still wake up feeling grateful that I get to live here. We talk to our kids a lot about gratitude. It's an easy way to plug into "happy" when you just need that little extra something. I don't feel grateful every day, of course. I mean, on the days that I slide on black ice from my back door into knee-deep mud on my way to the chicken house, I think I can be forgiven a few reservations. But generally I am delighted to live here every week that I can. At least a couple of times every single week I wake up with a feeling of gratitude the second I look outside my window. And I'm not alone.

Vermont is filled with romantics and people who want their kids in the woods instead of the malls. Folks come here from New York, Connecticut, New Jersey, and occasionally, at least in one case,

---

1. Let alone naked people filling water balloons at the hose.

2. Try paying your real estate taxes late, for just one tiny example. *They will print your name in the newspaper, for God's sakes.* Oh, and go into town without your bra? Fuhgeddaboudit.

from St. Louis, for a little Vermont magic. Life is old here. Well, it's probably old in lots of places, but here it is . . . a special old.

We have things like Town Meeting, early-American government still alive and contentious in the mountains. Instead of big-box stores, we have these quaint little country stores.[3] Along our roadways, there are small family farms where you can buy organic beef, raw milk, fresh eggs, and, for several months of the year, the freshest of vegetables. There are boutique dairies with every kind of cheddar, milky goat cheeses, and tangy blues.

There are lots of entrepreneurs here, too. Smokin' Bowls just off the Route 30 Stratton exit on VT 11 serves an apple-onion-smoked-cheddar-and-hard-cider soup to die for. You should probably try the Grafton cheddar and broccoli, as well. Oh, and the traditional chicken noodle, er . . . and the creamy tomato, if we're being honest. Pull over and grab a bowl. I promise that you'll come back.

And Up For Breakfast in Manchester, just one town away, is not to be missed. Bonnie has a rotating list of local specials which in various seasons include venison sausage that was probably running around the mountains just last month. There's the Vermonter, with local salty cured ham next to a short stack of maple buttery goodness that will hold you for a day or two at least. There is a turkey hash in the autumn that John swears by. I like a traditional Runny Benny with one fat blueberry pancake on the side. Those things are so bursting with local blueberries in August, they seem like cartoons. There's always a line, but it is so worth it. Besides, Bonnie will bring you a maple latte while you wait.

---

3. Yes. Yes, I know. I, too, read . . . and lived . . . it. But I do still think of them as quaint, actually. They are beautiful bits of Americana. When they aren't trying to kill you. I'm awfully glad they survive. Well, most of them. Mostly glad.

But maybe you're not hungry. Well, if you're in Pawlet, you should stop in to Lake's Lampshades. Judy Lake collects old fabrics and makes these beautiful French-inspired shades in thousands of patterns, along with her specialty lamps that are made from old Vermont postcards. Yes, postcards. Her lampshades are dripping with charm and panache. Decorators come from the chicest stores in Manhattan to stock up. And if you're into fiber arts, you can get wool from the sheep you watch grazing by the side of the road at a keen little shop on the corner in Almost-Any-Town, Vermont. You will find capes and shawls and blankets, spun and woven from these sweet, pastoral herds that dot our hillsides. Tourists pull over and take pictures of these bucolic little herds, practically all year long. Some of these wacky tourists even decide to move here and foster some of those sheep. Buy little stores. Make everyone in town angry. Possibly even write books about it. Crazy people. Anyway, they pack up their city lives and buy the little cottage next to the river. Or, in some cases, the old farmhouse at the bottom of the hill.

So, with all this tourism and entrepreneuring, we get a lot of folks that decide to move here from somewhere else. They decide to cash in their 401(k)s and make Vermont their home. To become real Vermonters. Well, to be frank, none of us manage the "real Vermonter" bit. Just ask anyone who has been here longer than you have. You're not a "real Vermonter" without a few generations behind you. You will remain a flatlander for the next hundred years or so. But we all feel that pull to try. To try to be a part of this beautiful place.[4]

---

4. I actually considered having a baby here just so I could produce an actual honest Vermonter of my very own. All this romantic beauty and baby fever go together really well. But I was forty something at the time, and for once I used a little bit of impulse control. Or John did. One of those.

Some folks retire here from someplace else. Others come with a plan. That plan might be to travel for work or to start a business or to work from home. Many newcomers are artists or writers. They can ply their craft anywhere, so they figure why not someplace so naturally beautiful? Others have been lucky in other businesses and figure that they will be here, too.

Of course, it is hard for the kids of these folks to stay, though. The beauty is . . . well, unencumbered by industry. It is hard for a lot of young people to figure out a job or to carve one out of nothing if they've never had one before. So our kids tend to graduate from college and then they gravitate to bigger cities.

But lots of them seem to come back when they have kids of their own. The idea of raising children in this sweet place is seductive. Ultimately it becomes all about figuring out the job thing. I think that will become easier as remote jobs take hold in the economy. People are starting to create regular jobs in regular far-flung companies that just have them commuting to their living rooms rather than into an office building. Still, the economics of making a living here is a puzzle to be solved.

Folks who have made the decision to come, though. Well, as they arrive they begin that familiar process of settling in. They want to become a part of the community. To figure out all the local customs. And that means all the obvious things, of course, like finding a doctor and a dentist. A lot of people think they will need a dry cleaner, but, as they quickly learn, most don't. At least not right away. Because no matter what time of year they come here, pretty soon it snows. And snow puts a damper on the whole silk-blouse-and-pressed-skirt party.

Oh, and shoes. I should probably mention the shoes. Shoes are the first things to go. Well, not altogether. We're not running around barefoot in the North Woods. I actually mean those gold lamé heels and red patent jobs. They are going to look pretty silly up here. You'll need to trust me on this. And you should instead stock up on boots. Muck boots for mud. Canadian boots for snow. These are necessities. Sandals? Well, it doesn't get warm enough for sandals until early June. And by warm enough, I mean that it is warm enough for a couple of hours a day. Okay, so maybe not "a day." Maybe, "some days." At any rate, the wardrobe adjustments are often a surprise to new arrivals. There are a few other surprises, as well. Some of them are even fun.

Raw milk? You bet. Raw milk.

I'll be honest about it. Raw milk sounded . . . almost . . . disgusting when I was shopping at the Whole Foods in St. Louis. I mean, I'd read all the warnings. Dire! Warnings! But then, one day I was passing the sign on the barn where I'd watched the cows wandering around their pasture every morning for a year. I drove past that field as I took the kids to school every day. And, you know, one day I just thought I'd stop in. For a second. Like you do.

MILK, the sign said. And just behind the barn was this whole field of sweet-looking black-and-white cows. I'm sure that's the species, Sweet Black-and-White Cow. It's a technical Vermont term. Anyway, back in May I watched as they came outside with their babies in tow. Mama cows and their calves all fresh and new and full of the joys of spring. The farmer always smiled and waved and I thought, What the heck? Let's see what this is about.

This happens pretty much identically all over Vermont. Every day. Well, wind and weather permitting. There is usually a door with a sign that says COME IN. Sometimes this door is on a barn, and sometimes it is right on the farmhouse. Then, there is a little room or an arrow pointing to the little room, where there is a refrigerator with a clipboard and a sign with a menu of the offerings. There is always milk—quarts or gallons—in glass jars. You pay a deposit for your first jar, and then just bring the empty jar back and exchange it for a full new one. Leave your money in the box before you go.

In addition to the milk, you'll sometimes get smaller jars of a thick, buttery-colored cream, and often there is yogurt, too. Most of these stands offer meat and eggs as well. Sometimes there are brochures about the benefits of raw milk, and the risk-reward charts always seem to fall heavily in favor of reward. Well, I guess they would. But I am a convert and what I can tell you is there is one main reward. That reward is the sublime, almost-ice-cream taste.

Raw cow's milk with a high butterfat content tastes like custard. Raw milk with lower butterfat content is like melted ice cream. The mouthfeel is rich. The texture is full. There are more flavor profiles in a stretch of Vermont dairy land than in any grocery store processed-dairy aisle. This is milk to the tenth power. It is heaven in a glass.

I always think of those "Got Milk?" commercials and imagine my own milky mustache. The way I see it, the cows graze on grass in my very own part of the world. They develop natural antibodies to local viruses and flu strains. I'd guess they pass those into their milk. Raw milk and local honey are a natural protection against disease. The raw-milk producers hardly use any pesticides or chemicals. At least not here in Vermont. There are food poisoning risks, sure. But, you know, I eat oysters raw. And I have raw eggs in my caesar dressing. And there's that steak tartare at Pastis. I mean, I agree that food poisoning is no joke when you are pregnant. But otherwise . . . well, it's a risk, but it's a small risk. And you really have to try this milk. A lot of people do. They seldom go back. And it's all part of being here in your new Vermont home, right? These are the sweet adjustments as you make your way through a state that has different customs, and a whole history built around a softer, country lifestyle.

ooooo

Of course, some adjustments are a bit more of a stretch. Like the guns, for instance. This is harder for me, but guns are part of the history up here, too. Lots of Vermont men hunt. The transplants tend to be bird hunters. Pheasant, turkey, woodcock, and grouse, mainly. They bird hunt with their designer dogs. Truth be told, we might be one of those families as well now. It's a little bit complicated. Benjamin has really taken to the outdoor life. He comes by it honestly. For as long as Benjamin could remember, Steve, his father, loved nothing so much as stalking around the countryside in safari gear. Generally he'd be sporting field glasses, but he was also a bit of an armchair hunter. So Benjamin has found, in the Vermont outdoors, a second home.

But there are other kinds of hunters, too. Real Vermonters, at least the ones that I know, fill their freezers with the meat they kill in the autumn. Deer and bear can feed a family well into the darker, colder months of winter. Sure there's a bit of sport to the hunt, but a lot of local families depend on the addition of a successful fall hunt to sustain them over a long winter. Initially most of the transplants seem a little shocked by all the shooting. The general stores all offer hunting licenses. You can't drive far in November without encountering a truck with a deer in the bed. It starts out as . . . unsettling.

But then, strangely enough, newcomers to Vermont often seem to have the odd sense that maybe, just maybe, they should learn to shoot, too. I mean, folks here . . . the Real Vermonters . . . have guns. All of them. And we've moved here to be Vermonters, after all. So maybe we should have a gun, too. Seems reasonable, yes? Anyway, this affects a lot of the men who move here. I mean, of course it does. But you'd be surprised at the women packin' as well.[5]

---

5. No, not me. Promise. I mean those little derringers tucked into a boot might be kind of sexy. But no one who knows me would even allow the conversation. They'd probably have me committed first.

Now, remember, these were people who in their old lives didn't even let their kids have toy guns. There were more than a few vegetarians. Gender-neutral non-warlike toys were the rule for these lefty liberals who loved Vermont. I mean, don't even let them get started on Barbie dolls. And, yet . . . guns? The real thing?

Well, it's not that they plan to shoot for sport or anything, but they start to think about predators in their yards. Those are the yards where their tiny, Manhattan-born poodles are hanging out. And then the notion that they are all alone in a house that's thirty miles from the nearest police station. Well, they've seen the movies. A gun. We need a gun. It seems like everyone up here has one. Why not me? It all starts to seem reasonable. Inevitable, even. Why not?

I could tell them why not. Just look at the accident statistics. But they are new to Vermont. Locals, of course, have figured this out. They've set up businesses that teach hunter safety classes and gun safety. The guys teaching those classes, Vermonters all, figure that these city people really need to learn what they are doing. Mostly, as it turns out, so they don't hurt anyone. Besides, after a few classes, the instructors sometimes get hunting-guide jobs. Generally, they just take the men in the group trout fishing. Sometimes there'll be a quail hunt. And there springs up another Vermont cottage industry. Guns and gun safety for the lefty blue city crowd.

Which is how my friends Ellen and Roger found themselves in a hunter safety class.

⟡⟡⟡⟡⟡

"I want a gun," Ellen announced one day, seemingly out of nowhere.

Roger greeted this with surprise, and a fair amount of resignation, which he did his best to hide. Ellen weighs about one hundred pounds soaking wet. She is a deeply intuitive intellectual. She is a psychoanalyst turned painter who grew up on the Upper East Side of Manhattan overlooking the park. She knew her ten or twelve blocks of Manhattan like the back of her hand. Vermont was not like Manhattan. But she was adjusting.

Roger grew up closer to the Bowery, down on the Lower East Side. He is a scrappy inventor/artist turned entrepreneur. He runs a successful tile and home décor company. They live in a beautiful spot along the Green River in a restored farmhouse with a glorious barn that houses their studios. Roger's company was in Middlebury at the time, and he was traveling a few nights every week. So Ellen was often all alone with her dog, Sophie, and cat, Cucina, and the pack of coyotes up on the hill. Well, the coyotes and the bears, who wandered down and mangled her bird feeders from time to time. Just the coyotes and bears. Oh, and there was a rabies epidemic. So, coyotes and bears. Possibly rabid coyotes and bears. She felt that Sophie would appreciate . . . well, really deserved . . . to have Annie Oakley, or similar, protecting her. There was actually a rabies epidemic at the time. Seriously. It was in the newspaper.

Now my dear Ellen loves the natural world, and she loves its animals best of all. She wouldn't hurt a spider in her house, much less shoot a bear or coyote in the woods. I know this. She knows this. But I imagine she was thinking that if worse came to worst, she would shoot up in the air and scare the varmint off. I mean if an honest-to-God gun-toting burglar came into Ellen's home she was way more likely to offer him tea in her grandmother's best china with a little honey and lemon on the side[6] than she was to shoot him. My friend Ellen is a gentle soul.

A gentle soul who now wanted to buy a gun.

Roger tried all the usual arguments, of course.

---

6. Unless perhaps he would prefer milk.

"Ellen, you could hurt yourself."

She countered with "Not if I'm careful. Everyone up here has a gun."

"But we don't know anything about guns," he said.

"Which is why I'll take a class. I can certainly handle a class. You may remember I'm a pretty good student.[7]

"But Ellen, we don't even believe in guns. We're liberals! What does this say about our politics?"

He tried. But it was, to be fair, halfhearted. He was gone a lot for work, so that was true. And besides, once Ellen set her mind on something there was little hope in changing it. He was a smart guy and this was a lesson learned years ago. Resistance was futile.

As luck would have it, Ellen's taxi driver, Phillip, had a gun for sale. Hmm, I'm not sure that sounded right. No, that's right. Phillip the cabdriver offered to sell Ellen a piece. I guess I should clarify a little.

See, Phillip had moved to Vermont a few years earlier and had started a car service called Manchester Taxi. He would pick us up at the airports and drive us and our assorted relatives back and forth between train stations and airports. And we had all gotten quite friendly with him on those long drives. I mean, you get to chatting. You get to know each other. Conversation meanders to coyotes and rabies and how one goes about picking up a piece, and pretty soon you're making plans to buy your cabbie's gun.

You know, like you do.

Anyway, Phillip had lived in Vermont long enough to have felt the need to buy a gun, but also long enough to get over it. Phillip showed up at Ellen's place with a rifle. It was a Winchester .30-30, which, for the uninitiated, is not a tiny gun. If you've ever seen John

---

7. A PhD, of course.

Wayne riding across the screen with the reins in his teeth and a rifle in his hands firing at bad guys, then you've seen a Winchester .30-30. It's a big gun. John Wayne was six feet four inches. Ellen is five feet notmuch. She could barely hold the thing, much less fire it.

Ellen took a look at these pretty little carvings on the stock, though, and said, "Yes indeed. It looks just about right." She bought it on the spot.

Minimally, Roger demanded that they should at least take some safety classes before they bought any ammunition. If they were going to be gun owners, they were going to be responsible gun owners. Now, as luck would have it, Ellen's lawyer friend from up the road, Mary Ann, and her lobbyist husband had been invited to go wild boar hunting in California. Wild boar.

It happens that the lobbyist husband had just inherited his father's gun collection. But he hadn't inherited his father's passion for hunting. Still, here he was in Vermont with a collection of guns. He guessed that now was probably time to learn how to use them. Mary Ann began looking for a class to get certified, so that they could fly to California to hunt boar. Well, honestly she hoped that they'd wind up in Wine Country with a little *cinghiale* on the table and a nice robust Kermit Lynch red Zin to go along with it. She began making inquiries, and finally she found Wynn.

Wynn owns a local landscaping business. He's a busy guy, but he also teaches hunter safety courses on the side.

"Mary Ann, I'd love to help, but it's a thirteen-hour course," he said. "I really can't take the time to do it for just one person. Not even two, really. Spring is almost here, and I have plants to get in and yards to spruce up. If you could find . . . say . . . six folks. That'd be enough to make it worthwhile."

"Six?" she asked. "You'd do it with a class of six?"

"Sure," he replied. "For a class of six, I'd do it."

Mary Ann knew that there were other transplants who would be eager to sign up. There must be, right? When you live in a place, you want what you see others doing. And she wanted to learn to shoot. It looked like fun. She was betting that lots of other people wanted to learn to shoot too. Maybe not boar. Or rabid coyotes. But, just to learn to shoot.

"Wynn, I'm sure I can get together a group of folks just like me. There has to be a bunch of us. I'll call you to schedule it."

"Okay," he deadpanned. "You let me know. I can hardly wait."

Of course, the first person she called was my friend Ellen. Perfect timing. It turns out that Mary Ann was right. There were a lot of people just like her. They found a lady dentist to add to their group. A dentist, Mary Ann the lawyer, and Ellen the psychoanalyst/painter. It was a class full of New Yorkers turned Vermonters. Well, a sort of Vermonter. They had the guns, anyway. Guns and overachieving advanced degrees. A small group of MDs, JDs, PhDs, and savvy entrepreneurs. With guns.

They made quite a crew.

As you can imagine, their classes were pursued with the same kind of determination that they had brought to their academic programs. They took notes. And asked questions. Lots of questions.

Wynn would say, "All right now, it's important to keep the safety on till you are ready to shoot."

The front row would ring out with "How come?" You know, come to think of it they were probably all in the front row, but you get the idea.

"Let's talk calibers," Wynn would continue.

"Yes, let's!" Ellen would eagerly chime in. "So, first of all, what's a caliber?"

Calibers, bullets, actions (bolts and levers), barrel life, tactics, and bore. They learned all about bore. Which incidentally has nothing to do with boar. Wild or otherwise. I know, I was surprised, too.

Anyway, they read everything they could between classes, and then peppered Wynn with questions. These were folks who knew how to do their homework. They were showing off their research and talking guns the minute they arrived. They were competitive and eager.

Pretty soon it was time for the test. Apparently, the course had both a written and a practical test for certification. Fine. This was a class of test takers.

Wynn informed them that the next time they met they'd have a three-hundred-question test covering the material in the course.

Roger may have asked first: "Three hundred questions?! Did we even learn three hundred things? How many do we have to get right to pass, Wynn?"

Wynn thought a moment and replied that "Well, now, the last group of boys I taught got seventeen right. I let 'em take it again, though. The second time they got about fifty." He may have scratched his chin at this point. "That was pretty good. And, 'sides, these boys could shoot, boy howdy could they shoot. So, I passed 'em."

Fifty?

Out of three hundred?

At any rate, our crew took their Vermont Hunter Safety test on the following Monday night.

They got the best grades in the history of the test. Of course they did. The not-to-be-named-in-this-book lowest-scoring participant made a 98 percent. And was shamed by that score. Next came the fieldwork, and by golly they all earned their hunter's patch, too. They were PhD-carrying gun-toting Vermonters now. Boy howdy.

ooooo

These Real Vermonters like Wynn are a big part of why I love Vermont. I love the newcomers, too, but the Real Vermonters teach us by example how to live well in this place. It is a good lesson for kids and adults alike. This is a place of simple beauty and it demands a plain response. You don't need colorful flags and banners when nothing could compete with the majesty of the landscape. Vermont does not need a decorator. The mountains are everywhere and right up close. There are no billboards. There are no strip malls. We have little country stores, instead. Everyone has a view here. There's even a view from the parking lot of the grocery store. It is America the way I imagine that America used to be. There are few people, and those that are here tend to be polite. You see, the thing about living in a place like this is that there is no anonymity to hide behind, so people tend to treat each other fairly. You may have a problem with your neighbor, land disputes are rampant here especially if you've built something that blocks the view, but always you are polite.

This civility isn't exactly unmotivated. That annoying neighbor might be the only person on the road the January night that you drive into a snowdrift. We have to help one another to live up here. It can be a harsh place for several months of the year, so there is a gentleness to our interactions as a community that city living doesn't share.

I miss things about the city, though. For one tiny little thing . . . can I just say? . . . I miss all that anonymity. There is nothing quite like going to a coffee shop in your sweats with messy hair and no makeup and reading the paper while you are on your third croissant with crumbs all over the table. That is not behavior you can manage in Vermont. You will see seven people you know and at least two will want to talk.

It is what it is.

Ten minutes after you move to Vermont, you will know every-body's business, and they will know yours. They will. Just watch. As soon as your kid goes to school, or you hire a plumber, or really if you just say hello. You are doomed.[8]

Okay, "doomed" might be a strong way to put it. But you cer-tainly ought to skip the affair with that cute guy down the highway. You will not be able to keep it a secret. Which is not to say that you'll feel the need to spread the word far and wide. You probably won't. But in the end, it won't matter. Everyone will know all about it.

Now, people do have affairs, of course. It's going to happen. But I always wonder if they really thought that we didn't all know. Like a small office or a school, there are just no secrets up here.

I mention this by way of context, you understand. About gos-sip. Because when the governor of Vermont asked me about Eli and the chair, I wasn't really prepared.

○○○○○

I'd been homeschooling Eli, my youngest, for years. We'd tried the local school after moving to Vermont, but found that it wasn't the right fit for us. Eli had been accustomed to the tiny classes at New City School, a great part of our life in St. Louis. New City's approach was based on Howard Gardner's theory of multiple intelligences, and it offered progressive education in a keenly intimate, nurturing environment. After the move, Hannah had been just fine at her high school, Long Trail, but Eli wasn't as suited to the local elementary. In the end, it just made sense to take up homeschooling, which, as it turns out, was dramatically more fulfilling than we would have guessed. John and I had found an easy rhythm and great comfort in

---

8. You might as well write a book.

being more a part of Eli's education. We had all felt a new joy in our relationships during that time. But then, well, Eli reached That Age.

Apparently when you reach the middle-school years, it begins to dawn on you that there are cooler people to spend your day with than your parents. So Eli had begun lobbying for a return to the more traditional school system. Seventh grade meant that he would be able to move into the independent country school that Hannah had attended. She had thrived there, and Eli decided that he was ready to make the move. He was a lot more ready for this than we were. Homeschooling had been all about love and learning. But he was smart and persuasive with what turned into a campaign, so we agreed that it was time.

For the most part, it worked out. Of course, Eli was a seventh-grade boy who had been homeschooled for quite a while. For him, the idea of school was mostly a place where you met other kids and planned basketball games, soccer games, skateboarding, and the like. This might have been a bit irritating to a few of the teachers who were, well . . . maybe a little shortsighted, in his view . . . about the goals of education. In the end, I'm pretty sure it didn't bother Eli that they hadn't come around to his more enlightened perspective. Surely they would in the end. Well, mostly.

John, who had enjoyed the homeschooling experience as much as I had, decided that it would be good to get involved at Eli's school. It started off as volunteering and coaching, but developed into a teaching position. This certainly wasn't the path he had expected to take, but if the Horrible Quaint Country Store had taught us anything, it was that you can't always predict where you'll end up.

Well, one day Eli was home sick. Sick sick. Like, pneumonia sick. And John called home from the school to check on him.

"Ellen, you should have been here. There was quite a performance," he chuckled. "The head of school called an assembly, and several teachers carried this office chair up on the stage that had been vandalized. It was pretty theatrical. Apparently, there was 'A Substance!' on the chair, and the head was offering amnesty if the perpetrators came forward. 'Amnesty?' Who knew he could be so dramatic?"

"Whose chair?" I asked with a teensy little jolt of concern.

"Ty's," he answered. "Looks like some kids came into the school over the weekend and did a little damage to it, poured soda or something on his chair. The way the head was acting, you'd think the 'Substance' was anthrax. I mean, go to the store and buy a little Resolve, for goodness' sake."

In John's telling of it, a hush had fallen over the assembly, as if the police had been called and were on their way. Presumably there would be CSI techs and blue lights and someone would *Get to the bottom of this!*

"Seemed like a bit of an overreaction," John added. "No one should be very surprised. I've heard these kids say that Ty is a complete jerk to them. They can't stand him."

Well, at least that's what he told me he said afterwards. In the aftermath. At the time, the word "Ty" had caused my vision to get a little blurry and my palms to sweat. I knew all about Ty. The math teacher.

My kid was one of the kids (there were a lot of these actually) who couldn't stand him. But, surely . . . not.

Besides, Eli had been at a birthday party over the weekend. Obviously I was buying into the whole police notion, because I was glad to realize he had an alibi. Er . . . didn't he? Because, I had just remembered that the birthday party was right down the street from the school. Surely not . . .

My Mom-sense was tingling.

"Eli??!!" I may have croaked. Well, in my sweetest Mom-voice.

The kid was really sick. An asthmatic with pneumonia and a 102 temperature is a sick kid. So I tried to lean on the Mom-voice rather than the Prosecutor voice. A little more June Cleaver than D.A. McCoy.

"Honey" (always best to start with "honey"), "Dad just called and he said the school held an assembly today. They carried Ty's chair up onto the stage and . . ."

And that was enough. I knew. I didn't have to keep talking. Moms know.

Eli looked out from under the covers with wide eyes and admitted, "I did it."

Well at least he wasn't shirking it. I guess that's good. I mean, a little mischief making isn't that bad.

"I peed on Ty's chair," he finished his confession.

What did he say?

Peed?

Did he just say peed?

Oh my God.

We had practically just sold the country store ten minutes ago. We were still recovering what reputation we had from having nearly ruined a town treasure. And now I was going to be the mother of the kid who peed on a teacher's chair. And it was Eli. Eli, who in thirteen years had been the easiest, the sweetest, most compliant kid. He never did anything much wrong. What the hell? Peed? Did he just say peed?!

This whole Vermont life was just not quite what I'd expected. We had moved here to have gentler village lives for our kids. We had definitely not moved here thinking one of them would start peeing in public. This was not going to be good.

Did I mention that John was teaching at this school?

With Ty?

The owner of the pee-soaked chair.

I called the head of school, right away. I put Eli on the phone and he owned up to the "offense." He asked for community service rather than amnesty. He knew his behavior was way out of bounds. Eli was a good kid. But he *was* a kid. His sense of justice apparently included peeing on a mean teacher's chair and then taking the punishment.

The way the kids saw it, this was a sort of justice. Ty reportedly spoke to them in an astonishingly condescending voice. Apparently, this had been righteously indignant pee. You know . . . sort of like peeing on a lawyer's chair. Or a dentist's. Perhaps it was not, in the grand scheme, all *that* horrible. But it was certainly not good.

Apparently, interviews were commencing. Eli called his best friend, Timmy, who had been along for the adventure. It had, after all, been his birthday party. Timmy, the good kid, had stayed outside the school. He didn't really think it was a good idea. Eli and a few others had gone in. I think my kid was the only "chair offender."[9]

I took on the grown-up call and talked to Tim's dad, Mike. Now, we love this family. Tim and Eli have been best friends since we moved here. These folks are a politically conservative Catholic family. We are a liberal mixed bag. But they love their kids just like we love ours. They had made our boy a part of their family just as we had gladly welcomed Tim into ours. But I worried about what they would think of the permissive parenting that had resulted in this messy episode.[10] I summoned up the courage and I made the call. After all, John had enough guts to face teaching at the school every day with Ty. So I agreed to take this one.

Tim's parents aren't scary folks. I mean, Peggy is just goodness

---

9. Real leadership qualities, there.

10. Truthfully, I wondered if it had.

personified. She is warm and kind. She always has been. If you run into her on the street, you just feel good for hours afterward. And Mike? Mike is a pharmacist who has been a teacher and a dad to six boys and one girl. He is funny and pragmatic, which is a pretty good combination. With seven kids, I'm sure he thought that he had seen it all. But, you know, I'm pretty sure he didn't often get calls about how his son's best friend committed some sort of bladder warfare at the middle school, while spending the weekend under his roof. That sort of thing had to be unusual. So I was a little nervous.

I dialed the number. Mike answered on the first ring. I had been hoping for Peggy.

"Hello."

"Hi, Mike. This is Ellen. I . . . I just wanted to call you and . . . uh . . . fill you in on the, er . . . situation."

And I did. In some detail. You know how sometimes when you're nervous you talk a little faster? Well, I talk pretty fast as it is. And a good bit, generally. So I'm not sure if he took in everything I was saying, but to be honest the awkward pauses where I was looking for new ways to say "peeing" and "sorry" probably gave him room to breathe. Finally I reached what could only be the end of the explanation. And I knew that now was the moment. This is where he would react. Maybe he would forbid Eli from visiting his house. Who knows, really? This was not a situation any of us knew just how to deal with. I had no idea what to expect.

The line was silent for a second (presumably making sure I was done rattling on) and I could hear Mike take a breath. He said, and I will never forget this so long as I live, "Thanks for calling, Ellen. You gotta wonder what that teacher did to make a kid want to pee on his chair."

I loved this man. I loved him and his whole family. I wanted to nominate him for Nicest Guy Award or something.

And I was surely with Mike on this one. I gotta say, it made me wonder too.

ooooo

So there I was at an event for the governor and he asked me, "Ellen, hi, aren't you the woman whose kid peed on the chair?"

He asked good-naturedly. He did. Because he's a friendly guy, and I'm guessing he was hoping for a new detail on the story, given that he was going to the source. But he, the governor of the great state of Vermont, asked about my son's penchant for . . . political urination.

Privacy, yes. Anonymity, no. It's just part of life up here. But if you pee on a chair at school, you've pretty much given up on privacy. And anonymity is too much to ask for. Secrets in Vermont? Not so much, really.

Boy, we really needed a vacation.

ooooo

BACK AT THE TABLE

We needed a vacation, yes. And we needed comfort. All of us.

There was the pee-er who caused the whole thing in the first place. He was a folk hero of sorts, but even being a folk hero among young teenagers can take its toll. Eli could not go anywhere without someone asking him about the C H A I R. And, of course, he also had teachers and their combined opinions to experience. John had to teach at that school every day next to the guy who had suffered the affront. Peed-on Chair Guy had friends on the faculty. So did John, of course, and they seemed to be lining up on opposing sides. On the one side was a teacher who'd suffered the indignity of having his chair violated. On the other side was the beleaguered father of the pee-er, husband of a school board member, who was mainly just trying to coach and teach and keep his head down.

And then there was me. I was out in the world acting as the PR advance team for the family. On some days I was shameless, and heaped barely concealed barbs on the math teacher. On other days I was embarrassed, and offered a wounded face to the world. The day I ran off the snow-covered road into a ditch and the tow guy asked me about the chair was not one of the good days.

We had pancakes for supper that night. Salty buttermilk and blueberry. Eli asked for (and got) chocolate chips in his. We had just started to relax from all that sugary buttery goodness, while talking about an upcoming dance, when the syrup dispenser lost its cap. Syrup got everywhere. I mean, everywhere. It was on all the cushions, the pillows, dripping into the cracks of the table. We used up masses of paper towels. In truth, we were mostly just smearing it all around. The smell of maple filled the house. It was on our clothes and in our hair. The dogs were licking the stuff off the floor and their muzzles were sticky for days after.

Eli was the first one to start laughing a little. Then I sat down right in the middle of the floor and joined in. John tipped the almost-empty bottle of syrup back and guzzled what was left.

"I should have just poured syrup on his chair," Eli said. "That would have been way more of a Vermonty insult and I bet no one would have even cared."

And with that, with gooey syrupy fingers and floors, in that one instant, we all moved on. People must still have mentioned the chair from time to time but I honestly don't remember. What I remember is that night at the table.

I remember the smell of dark rich maple and the sound of laughing. I remember thinking, He's thirteen years old, for goodness' sakes. He's practically Tom Sawyer.

And Ty, the math teacher? Well, now I was thinking of giving him a jar of syrup for Christmas . . . maybe one with a broken top.

CHAPTER FOUR

The Pond

"ELLEN, WE DO NOT OWN A BUS."

John was surveying the room where I had staged the things that needed to be packed into our cars. We were going on vacation. Vacations have always been a core value in this family. When I was a little girl growing up in Granite City, Saturday was library day. Really, that was where it had started.

My mother was one of those ladies with a weekly beauty-shop appointment. Every Saturday, like clockwork, my mom would head to the beauty shop. I came along, but mostly for what happened after the primping and setting. My mom and I would leave her beauty-shop appointment and head straight for the town library, where we would both check out bags of books. My dad died when I was just five, so my mom and I spent a lot of time together. Just the two of us most of the time. Luckily we both loved to read, and, maybe more importantly, the library was free. The only library rule at our house was that you couldn't choose more books than you could carry.

On those Saturdays, I leaned toward novels about far-flung places. Phoebe Atwood Taylor's Cape Cod mysteries were favorites of mine in middle school. It was in that library, with a friendly librarian named Jean who ordered Ms. Atwood Taylor's books from the other libraries in our system and saved them up for me, that I hatched my plan to get to the Cape. Jean had a multicolored bean-bag chair where I would plop down, begin reading, and start dreaming about future trips.

As a mom, I meant to take my kids to all those places I had always dreamt about. I knew how the stories had broadened my own worldview. I could only imagine how much the actual travel would open up theirs. So vacation had always been as important to our lives, and to our parenting, as supper at the table. It felt essential. When our kids were little, we would save up all year for the annual trip. The kids helped us plan for it as a sort of game, too. On our trip, everyone was responsible for one day. We each were in charge of the activity for that day, where and what we ate, and making sure that the whole family was taken care of. It was a game, but it was also an exercise in planning. It became a tradition for us. A tradition that's in our family DNA.

This year we decided that we were renting a house on Martha's Vineyard for an extended stay. I had snagged a client out there, so I would be working on the island for a hunk of the summer. It seemed like a nice way to incorporate a longer vacation into regular life.

Now, as I kept explaining to Mr. We Don't Own A Bus, packing for a house that you will actually live in isn't like packing for a trip. This wasn't a hotel event. It wasn't even a couple of weeks in a rental cottage. I would be working while we were there, so I needed all the trappings of my work life. That meant shoes, purses, clothes, a briefcase, jewelry, computers, and files. In fact, I needed more clothes than I usually would. There were formal business-related fundraising events that I was expected to attend. So, even more clothes than normal. But it wasn't really the clothes that had John shaking his head. His problem might have been with the bedding.

We had rented a house on Ice House Pond in West Tisbury. Ice House Pond was an island source, oddly enough, of ice at the turn of the twentieth century. Now it was just a natural treasure. The cottage in the woods came with four bedrooms and seven beds. All of those beds would be full most of the time that we stayed there.

And a full bed needs dressing. It's just simple math. On top of that, earlier in the summer the island can still be chilly at night. So that meant comforters, which no matter how many times you sit on, or how many boxes you pile them under, always seem to puff right back up again.[1] But after a second, I realized that he wasn't staring at the comforters. He must have accommodated himself to the bedding. The headshaking seemed to be about the large pile of fabric he was standing over. A few . . . just a few, really . . . colorful quilts . . . and tablecloths . . . stacked next to a box of candles.

"Look," I said, "it's a plain little cottage. We cannot spend months of our lives without color."

Well, I suppose we could, but I wasn't about to say so. Besides, vacations are supposed to be fun, and I wasn't planning on starting this one out in black and white.

"But El," he . . . I hesitate to say "pleaded" . . . but he questioned carefully, "what about all these candles? Do we *really* need all of those?"

He started counting off the reasons that those candles weren't all that important.

"We have to fit inside the car too, you know. We can't stick the dogs in the trunk. And don't forget the cat. She's going in the carrier, but we really can't mash anything in next to that . . ."

As he ticked off the troubles, he started wandering around the house muttering at things I'd stacked up for packing.

"What is this . . . ?" And that went on for a while. He would walk from pile to pile muttering. It's a thing he does.

Oh, blah. Blah. Blah. We could manage. John can pack a car better than anyone I've ever met. I don't know why he always feels

---

1. And if they didn't we'd probably have to get new ones. They *are* comforters, after all. Puffy is sort of the point.

the need to do this bit, where he walks around muttering about how it can't be done. He always managed. Yes, I may have packed a bit . . . enthusiastically . . . but he always found a way to make it work. Besides, we would be taking two cars, and I figured I could sneak some scarves in between the folds of those comforters. I'd already hidden a box of pans behind the chair. That was a little unwieldy, though. Maybe I could stick those pans in the folds of the comforters, too. They were already puffy.

Oh, and I hadn't even gotten the condiments out yet. We needed to take the good balsamic. Sure there were lots of shops on the island, but the prices were astronomical. Gas was always a dollar more than at home, and balsamic could cost you more than double what you paid for it in Vermont. So, really I was doing us all a big favor by packing it. Besides, there was plenty of trunk space. Now really, how hard could this be?

We were going to need all this stuff. The cottage had one main room that was kitchen, dining area, and living room, with a charming woodstove in the center next to a primitive staircase. Most of the space was dominated by a big table. It wasn't an antique, or in any way interesting. It was just big. The kitchen area was open to everything else and featured a wall of rather drab wooden cabinets. There were also some drab beams. Drab was kind of a theme. It was, after all, a rental.

The couches in the living room were pretty basic too. They would need pillows and colorful throws. One of the nicest features of the place was the wall of sliding glass doors that opened out onto the cedar deck . . . which, now that I mention it, was a huge expanse of old weathered wood. Weathered wood has its own beauty, but not a lot of color. Atop that sat a huge, weathered, colorless picnic table. So, you know, *boring*. The place was screaming for color and softness.

Make no mistake about it, though, we were thrilled to get this place in all its cozy drab glory. Months of calls and research had finally resulted in this little cabin right on the pond that would let us come with our dogs. Okay, sometimes there might be three dogs, but we got permission for two. We left the cat out of the conversation. And, really, if a guest brought a dog we'd have to welcome them, too. It would be rude to turn them away. And Benjamin was in his early twenties, so that really made him a guest, I would argue. He was only coming weekends. So minimally, he could be called . . . seasonal.

Pippi didn't count, in my view. Pippi was Hannah's Moodle. Well, sort of. She had been a Christmas gift to Hannah years earlier, but now she lived with us mostly full-time. We all adored her, Hannah most especially. But Hannah's college dorm probably had a no-Moodle clause, so Pippi lived back at home with us. She was the twenty-pound alpha in the pack. And she was a Vermont girl through and through. So it was kind of like taking on a grandchild who just hadn't been officially adopted. Anyway, I didn't think she needed to be stipulated in the lease since *technically* the adoption paperwork had never been formalized and she only weighed twenty pounds besides. Tiny. Hardly even a dog.

There were about a dozen houses on the pond hidden deep into the woods. Several of them had lovely water views. Ours was one of those.[2] The big airy master bedroom had the best view, and when I imagined working up there or out on the deck, my heart sang. I had been thinking about this pond literally all year long. Most of my clients are schools and colleges, so summer is slow. I had found work to do during the summer on the island, as the wardrobe that John was fretting over would show, but working with so many schools meant that I got a form of summer vacation, too.

Anyway, there was one especially lovely island family filled with a bunch of smart, practical women that owned four or five of the

---

2. I should probably not say "ours," but it really felt like we were connected to that cottage.

houses that were directly on the pond. They rented some of them, and one of the sisters was amenable to pets. In fact she loved dogs. I immediately loved her too. And luckily, our dogs had great island references. We had been renting for a couple of years, and people generally liked our dogs more than they liked us.

Plus, I tended to have the cottages we rented steam-cleaned thoroughly when we left. There would be nary a hair left behind. The houses were sometimes better off when we left than before we came. So, anyway, we were thrilled to get this particular house on the pond, even if it was a little . . . drab.

I was imaging the loons telling us goodnight, early-morning swims, maybe Eli would fish in a canoe. There was a dock down on the private end of the pond. It floated out into the pond. I pictured racing the kids to the dock. I'm a good swimmer, so I was going to show them a thing or two.

But there was still the house to consider. It was a functional rental, nothing more. It had the pond, which was all I really cared about. But I knew we were going to fill it to bursting with our particular brand of family, so it had better have a calming vibe. You might not know this, but I do not have a naturally calm personality. I tend more toward . . . excitable.

So do Benjamin and Hannah.

Eli is a bit more like his dad than the others. *A bit.* The rest of us, though, we make up for the lower volume. The house was going to need softening around the edges. And color. And my belief is always that yards and yards (and yards) of fabric by candlelight can be the answer to this particular problem.

So I had an old bohemian quilt with deep reds and purples, some summery green, and shots of goldenrod. It was a mix of patchwork patterns. It had cotton and silk top-stitching and was a perfect topper for the picnic table on the deck.

I'm a scarf person. I have hundreds of shawls, scarves, and pashminas. When I check into a hotel room, I drape scarves over the lamps. It adds a warm, feminine vibe to what would otherwise be a cold and impersonal room. I think scarves are comforting and sexy all at once.

I have a funky blue-and-white cotton scarf that is a giant square. I imagined that if I folded it into a big triangle it would be perfect in the middle of the dining room table. Then I could top that with a curvy vase full of roadside wildflowers.[3] The room would warm right up.

"Ellen, this will not all fit," said the cold voice of reason. "Come on, honey, there must be pots and pans in the rental."

I appealed to reason. "Do you really want to try to make an omelet with some crummy pan you've never seen before? It'll probably be flaking Teflon into our food."

"Well, you have to take *something* out," he countered. "There are seventeen candles in here. Is there some magic significance to seventeen?"

He had me there. I was actually surprised that there were only the seventeen. He must not have found the tapers or their holders yet. I had hidden them in the pillowcases with the pillows for protection. See, I was thinking ahead. Every bedroom was going to need candles. And the bathrooms too, of course. I thought that the outdoor shower would be prettier with some hanging candle jars, and then there was the living room . . . kitchen . . . and the dining table. I pictured my scarf on the table with the flowers in the middle and candles on either side. I could probably make what was a dreary little centerpiece into something quite pretty. Oh, and the deck. The picnic table would need candles. And now that I was thinking about

---

3. Oh! I had to find a place in the cars for the vases.

it, I could really use some votives for the deck railings. That could be a twinkling nighttime space. That would pull folks out onto the deck so that we didn't all crowd around in the kitchen. It could be a small space with all of us inside. Best to think ahead.

John kept wandering and muttering. "Knives? Knives?!"

"When Benjamin starts catching fish, do you plan to try and make sushi à la butter knife?" I was glad to have the reasonable high-ground here.

Mutter mutter mutter . . . "Something's just got to give here," he repeated. Again.

On the morning when we finally climbed into our overburdened cars, it was still dark outside. We were aiming for an 11:00 AM boat, and then lunch on the island. That meant that we had to be on the road by 5:00 AM just to be safe. We had to budget in stops for the dogs, and Friday's weekend traffic out of Boston headed for the Cape. Eli and I were in one car with the cat and the bedding and . . . well, a lot of stuff. John had the dogs, the suitcases, and, truth be told, a lot more stuff. At the last minute, I ran back into the house and came out carrying a big glass vase with hand-painted butterflies on it with a bundle of purple candles tucked inside. The candles were wrapped inside napkins. I thought it was a clever use of space. John thought . . . well, actually John drove away muttering and sent a spray of rocks up as he went. I tucked the vase between some colorful pillows and we were off.

Eli slept through the sirens. And the slowing down. And the pulling over to the side of the road. John was ahead of me, and as far as I could tell didn't see me pull over either. Maybe the muttering was fogging up his side mirrors. I started to call him, but thought that maybe I'd just see what this was all about first. No need to get the lawyers involved at the first sign of trouble. I hadn't been speeding. I knew that. And I was pretty sure that my license plates were okay. The inspection stickers were good. Maybe I just burned out a light or something.

I rolled down my window and the police officer started with "Ma'am." Nothing good is going to follow when the police officer starts with "Ma'am."

I'm pretty sure that this is when Eli woke up, but kept his eyes closed. I know this now, because at our next dog stop, he made quite a performance out of repeating the whole conversation to his dad.

"Did you see Mom get stopped by that cop?" He was certainly wide-eyed now.

"He told her that all her windows were blocked, and that she couldn't possibly see, and that she was a road hazard." That part seemed particularly funny to him.

"She started telling him all about the house and how you yelled at her about all the stuff. Pretty soon they had the trunk open and he was in there rearranging everything. He told her that the pillows could go under the seats. I think maybe she invited him to the island."

John just smirked.

Well, even with the smirking and the rearranging we made it.

ooooo

The Bourne Bridge, which connects the Cape to mainland Massachusetts, is a line of demarcation. It is where the happy holiday feeling kicks in for us every single time. There is a giant smiling lobster gracing a restaurant just on the other side of the bridge. He brings his own special brand of silly happiness to the cars passing by. There are trimmed topiaries at the first rotary that spell out "Cape Cod." That's all it takes. As soon as we see that, we burst into song.

"We're going to the Cape. We're going to the Cape. Heigh-ho the derry-o we're going to the Cape!" This may have been a teensy bit more appropriate when the kids were younger. At three it was adorable. At eight it was delightful. In their twenties and our not-twenties . . . well, it must be said that at least we all know the lyrics a lot better now.

When we start seeing signs for Woods Hole, there is a special sense of anticipation. I always anxiously look to see if the ferry is in the slip. It usually is, but seeing it there is a thrill. We get in line, then get out and stretch the dogs until we are invited to board. We drive on, parking our car in the impossibly tight quarters of an always full-to-bursting summer ferry. The traffic directors are pros. They get us all on quickly, time after time. They make room for that extra-long truck or that just-one-more beggy standby passenger. I have been that beggy standby passenger[4] and I am always grateful for the professional and cheerful way that I am treated. I have never been made to feel guilty for my lack of foresight. These folks seem to know that stuff happens. Sometimes you just have to get on or off the island unexpectedly. The ferrymen[5] view the standbys as one more challenge. And mostly, they get the job done. The Steamship Authority guys are good-humored and mightily efficient.

The Vineyard comes into view just a minute after the ferry pulls out. We savor the sea air from the top deck, watching the gulls float alongside. They are probably hoping for errant popcorn or sandwich crust. Sometimes we oblige. When the wind blows my hair back and I tilt my head to the spray, I remember Jean at the Granite City Library and say a little silent prayer of gratitude. The transit is a quick forty-five minutes. When the arrival whistle blasts, we trundle the dogs back to the car and begin the island adventure.

Like Vermont, the island is unmarred by big commercial signs.

---

4. I'm sure that's a shock.

5. I say "men" because they always are. I have never once seen a woman doing this essential island work.

Occasionally there will be a small hand-lettered sign offering flowers for sale by the side of the road. Sometimes the sign is for fresh eggs. Those signs just add to the charm. There is a subtle beauty to the island's wooded farm lanes, in contrast to the dramatic glory of the seaside. The roads we take follow rolling farmland and short, dense island woods through wild roses, beach plums, daisies, and lilacs early in the year. The blueberries and lilies come as the summer opens up. The weathered, silver-gray shingled cottages sit amid woods and next to quiet salt ponds in every village. You can hear the gentle soft murmurs of the Sound on one side of the island and the pounding waves oceanside. The Vineyard is only twenty-five miles end to end. The sounds and smells of the sea surround you.

On this trip, we were headed to the pond cottage, which is tucked way out in the woods in one of the five local villages on the Vineyard. Each of those villages has a personality.

First, down island there is Edgartown. It is easily the fanciest village. Think Kennedy. Think pink-and-green Lilly Pulitzer women and charming rows of ship's-captain-styled houses with picket fences and roses trailing everywhere. Really. Everywhere. Now imagine a harbor with an old, genteel lighthouse, shops, restaurants, and the light smell of salt on the air. The houses here are expensive but not the huge, ostentatious McMansions of the dot-commers. Here, the houses are filled with simple gleaming wood floors and fireplaces that get put to good use. These homes are gracious and old . . . like the money.

In Edgartown, there is a grand hotel called the Harbor View. Its wide front porch is generously, but not overly, filled with rocking chairs, which are just perfect for reading and watching sailboats bounce around the harbor.

The restaurants? Well, Atria's funky basement-bar burgers are legendary. John loves the Thai shrimp burger. Eli favors the Fast Eddie, with a softly fried egg on top. Atria's even has an especially decadent foie gras burger. Chef Aaron Zeender always runs the best-loved island spots. They have faithfully kept his menu in the restaurant upstairs. You can even still get his caesar with a tiny deep-fried quail egg or his braised short ribs that, honest to God, actually melt in your mouth. The herb-crusted wok-fried lobster is a singular experience. The place is amazing. If you need a wonderful cappuccino afterwards, Espresso Love is the best coffee garden around. The cappuccino is fantastic, and dogs are welcome. Enough said.

Next up is the port town of Oak Bluffs. OB was an affluent African American playground in the mid-twentieth century. There is a Methodist campground in the center of town with a beautiful tabernacle surrounded on all sides by adorable gingerbread bungalows. Oak Bluffs is one of the two ferry towns, and as a wet town on a mostly dry island, it's the one that most of the day-trippers go to. Its downtown area has all the fudge and ice-cream shops you could hope for, and the oldest carousel in America. If you're thinking painted ladies, cotton candy, and gorgeous ocean views, then you've just about got it.

The other ferry town is Vineyard Haven, inside West Tisbury, smack in the middle of the island. VH is dry, so the day-trippers tend to skedaddle. It's an upscale hippie town. If there is such a thing. Carly Simon's Midnight Farm store is here. It's sort of a cooler version of Anthropologie. In Vineyard Haven, high-end bohemian fashion[6] mingles with hip coffee shops, next to Bunch of Grapes Bookstore.

The Black Dog Tavern is a popular spot for tourists looking for a cup of chowder and great indoor harbor views. It has a giant fireplace and wide windows that feed the island theme. Locals are supposed to smugly think of it as a tourist trap. Fine. Let them. I am glad to be trapped here on a rainy afternoon. That mug of chowder

---

6. Alley Cat is one of the best. I can come here looking like something the tide dragged in and still leave feeling beautiful.

with the big croutons is what I start craving when the first raindrops fall. Give me a good stormy fog and I will be wrapped in a shawl, looking at the sailboats and daydreaming from one of those windows every single time.

West Tis is where rolling farmland meets beach in an almost (but not quite) secluded extension of the bohemian life downtown. Lambert's Cove and Ice House Pond are both in West Tis. So is Long Point, which is a protected nature preserve. Ospreys nest on tall poles built just for them. West Tis has a farmers' market twice a week in summer, and an old country store called Alley's. There's always good island produce and local cheese at that store. They've got coffee, pastries, and the newspapers a New Yorker or Bostonian might need. They really do seem to have everything. We even like the country store in West Tisbury. Imagine that. West Tis is Vermont with beaches.

The up island village of Chilmark is home to long, windswept beaches and gorgeous farms. Those yummy dark-chocolate-covered blueberries and cranberries you may have tasted come from Chilmark Chocolates. You can get pizza by the slice and eat it on the wide front porch at the Chilmark Store when the trip back home is too long to wait for supper. Lucy Vincent Beach is in Chilmark, and so is Great Rock. Jackie O lived here, and so do folks with several million to spend on a house and a craving for an island vibe.

Finally, Menemsha is the little fishing village made famous in the movie *Jaws*. The commercial fishing boats and pleasure craft tie up side by side in a charming tableau that gets photographed all summer long. This is where everyone goes for fresh fish. Those fish are caught an hour or so before being wrapped in newspaper for you to take home. Lobster rolls are no-frills here, with just bread and butter for dressing. I've seen people carry whole lobsters and a cup of butter to their beach blankets to watch the sunset. The fishermen work alongside the tourists in what seems like a timeless ritual of keeping us full. Sometimes a sudden storm will blow in here. The beachgoers huddle under rain gear with hoods pulled tight. But they wait. Because on this island, the rains come and go and are replaced by sunshine and glimmering blue-violet seas in a fast hurry.

At the tippy top of the island is the Gay Head beach and lighthouse. Gay Head is known, now, by its proper Indian name, Aquinnah. This is where the nude beaches are. Okay, actually nudity is legally prohibited here, but tolerated. Unlike at Lucy Vincent, where nudity is legal but not socially accepted. This is a fairly well known island rule.[7]

Gay Head has the most dramatic of the red-clay cliffs on the island. I've been a lot of places, and there is hardly a prettier place in the world than Gay Head. The water is deep navy, melding into a teal-turquoise in the summer months. The juxtaposition of blue sky, red clay, and jewel-colored water is breathtaking. Seagulls, seals, and craggy rocks. It is pure glory.

We discovered Ice House Pond through Hannah and Benjamin. They had gotten to know the island over the time that we'd spent there. Ice House had recently been opened to the public by the conservation-minded Land Bank. Four carfuls of people could come at a time and park in a tiny wooded lot. The visitors could then tramp down the blueberry-covered path and swim in the pond. There were a bunch of posted rules, though. I've never been a big fan of posted rules. Shocking, but true. Still, everyone we talked to swore that the pond was "Amazing!" Our dear friend Sarah Hibler had taught both her babies, Jasper and Clementine, to swim there. She and her partner, Aaron, both urged us to go, and they are island people whose beauty standards are very high.

So I was curious. It was just a pond. It wasn't connected to the

---

7. It's a little comforting to know that the whole island has naked rules. Just like our house.

ocean. It wasn't a saltwater pond. It was . . . a pond. Still, we thought we should give it a try. We parked at the pond and were immediately grilled by the ranger. The ranger?

"Can you folks all swim?" Well, I guess that's a decent rule. There probably isn't a lifeguard on the pond, and best to be safe.

"Yes," we agreed that we could all swim.

The ranger gave us a bit of a sideways look and asked, "You aren't coming here to sunbathe are you?"

"Well, no," we answered.

"And no picnicking. No food or drinks. Or nudity. You can take your towels in, but nothing else." Well, all right then . . . no tuna salad sandwiches in the buff. Got it.

"You don't have any dogs, do you?" he asked somewhat suspiciously. Maybe he could just tell we were dog people.

"Well, not in the car."

It was a strange welcome. Usually the island was such a friendly place. Up island, particularly, was always friendly. This was odd.

"All right, you'll jump off the dock, but no diving . . . just jump . . . and then begin swimming immediately. There is no standing near the bank. The plants around the bank are fragile and are protected."

I felt like I should respond, "Sir, yes, Sir!"

By the time he was finished, I almost didn't want to go.

But we'd come all this way. And everyone had said such nice things about the place. So I was game. And then . . . well, then we came to the end of the path. And, oh my. I hardly owned any words.

It was like stepping onto a movie set marked *Island Pond*. The island was already really really good. This is where it got great.

Ice House Pond sits in the middle of a secluded piny wood. It is a ten-acre freshwater pond formed by glaciers and is spring-fed. The smell is the first thing you notice. It is this mix of pine and fresh water and sunshine on trees. A heady mix.

I looked up and saw ospreys diving from their seemingly

impossibly high nests at the top of an old-growth pine into the pond and then back again. On our first visit, we didn't hear the loons, but they were there. I knew that one day I would wake up to their calls. I knew this down to my toes.

I just knew.

We dove in and swam to the other side of the pond. Slowly. When we got to what we thought was the middle, we all stopped to catch our breath. A turtle popped his head up, looked us over, and seemed to decide that we were okay before he ducked back down.

Which prompted Eli to ask, "What, is he the water ranger?" We giggled and splashed and dove under the surface. We couldn't believe our luck. This place seemed untouched by time, or humans. Of course, we knew it wasn't. We'd just met Mr. Don't Stand On The Bank Ranger up top. But this was a pristine example of New England pond, and the whole island was intent on keeping it that way.

Fine by us.

ooooo

We all love the beaches and islands of New England's coast. We've been coming for years. I had eventually grown up, and had tracked down Phoebe Atwood Taylor's favorite spots from all those books I'd read as a kid. She was right. There was a lot to love here.

On the island, people don't have to lock their doors. It's a lot like Vermont that way. You never hear the annoying sounds of car alarms, because most folks just leave their keys in their cars.[8] I've never seen a car sidelined without someone immediately stopping to offer help. Every hitchhiker gets a lift quickly. Usually these are teenagers who have missed a bus. They look worn and beach-raggled. It's almost impossible to take a walk on the main roads without someone stopping to offer you a lift. Even the people seem to be prettier here.

---

8. Admittedly, this might just mean that they've been quietly stolen. That's a mixed blessing.

Maybe it's the lens of the vacationer, but island faces are often weathered and welcoming. Or maybe it's because everyone smiles here.

And just like Vermont, the nighttime is especially quiet. There is a velvety stillness that wraps itself around the island. Beachwalkers hoping to catch a sunrise will hear muted foghorns in the distance and the occasional whistle of fishing boats headed out for the day through morning mist. But even these seem soft and quiet, like the lapping of the darkened waters. Since way back when we lived in St. Louis, the Cape had been our favorite summer vacation spot. Possibly Eli loves it best of all, though. He has sort of grown up here. Summers on the island were where he discovered the joys of sand and surf, oysters, learned about boats, tides, fishing, and living in a small island community. He also, it should be noted, got into his share of . . . well, not exactly trouble . . . but, colorful memories. He has broken into hotel pools with a happy band of marauding teenagers, hitchhiked across the island, and happened on a Russian "filmmaker" with a crew of "actresses" filming an X-rated film by the pool of our hotel. Not a hotel he'd broken into, mind. We had a claim on that particular hotel pool. It was the film crew that had broken in that time. We decamped from that pool pretty quickly, though the auteur might have exited even faster. I'm not sure Eli took in quite everything that was going on, but it remains one of his proudest moments. Oh, and he met Larry David. But when you are a boy, Larry just isn't going to compare to stumbling into the middle of a poolside porn scene.[9]

When Eli was young he didn't much care where we vacationed as long as it included a beach. He was probably three or four when we started coming to the Vineyard. Back then, we stayed at the Harbor View. Its teal porch rockers are just across from Lighthouse Beach, on the eastern tip of the island.

---

9. Frankly, I'd bet that Larry David would agree.

Lighthouse Beach features a beautiful lighthouse built in the late nineteenth century, at the height of the whaling industry. Of course, it wasn't actually built on this beach. The original 1828 lighthouse didn't survive the 1938 hurricane that hit the island. The Coast Guard took over the Lighthouse Service in 1939 and planned to build a new beacon on a skeleton tower. However, the town couldn't imagine putting a new twentieth-century structure on its classic lighthouse beach, so an enterprising Coast Guard came up with a happy solution. It moved (by barge) a vintage 1881 lighthouse from Ipswich and reinstalled it here. The beacon is simple, beautiful, and quintessentially New England.

The beach surrounding the lighthouse is not really a swimming spot, but it is a rocky area containing tide pools filled with crabs and, as it turns out, sand sharks. You see, there is apparently a longtime tradition of little boys and little girls playing in these tide pools by tying raw chicken to the ends of sticks and holding them in the water. The sticks. Not the children.

The chicken-stick crowd are apparently a secret society of some sort. Unsuspecting parents bring their kids to look at the lighthouse and before you know it older kids are teaching the newcomers how to catch crabs and dodge jellyfish. John and I read books in deck chairs for many summers as Eli became commander of Lighthouse Beach.

One Independence Day I remember particularly well. Eli must have been eight or nine. We had spent the day eating lobster rolls and BBQ while watching the town parade. I had commandeered[10] a much-coveted round table on the porch for our family to watch fireworks later in the evening. I had tended the table and chairs all day, while sending John and the bigger kids out to the beaches after

---

10. Well, our boy was the commander.

the parade. I had a juicy Daniel Silva thriller and Eli had two pounds of raw chicken in a bucket. We couldn't have been happier.

John, Benjamin, and Hannah got back in time for supper and we all took turns coax-feeding Eli. We'd wander out to him while he was surrounded by the troops and convince him that he had time for a bite of clam. He had a dozen boys fishing right alongside him, and they had caught (and let go) about a hundred crabs. He had a bucket of seahorses, crabs, and creatures we couldn't name. It was quite a bucket of adventure.

As the night began to darken, thousands of people made their way onto Lighthouse Beach without us really noticing. The big fireworks display was going to be just there, and of course folks wanted to get a nice view. Eli was happily lost in the tide pool medley, and he couldn't be enticed to the porch for the fireworks by lobster roll or clam strip. Children were arriving in the dozens, so Eli's audience—and troops—were multiplying faster than anyone could keep up with. Only, then the fireworks started. You know, the reason that everyone was here. Well, everyone but Eli. Eli was here for the tide pools.

A thing we didn't know, and that wasn't covered in our little tide pool guidebook, was that fireworks scare crabs . . . and seahorses . . . and the other little mysterious creatures that Eli was putting in his bucket. Also, those big booms scare the significantly larger creatures swimming just offshore. Creatures that hurried into the tide pools as fast as their fins could carry them. Creatures like the four- . . . six- . . . I don't know, maybe fifty-foot-long sand shark that Eli caught on a stick.

A stick.

With raw chicken . . . and a stick.

Everyone nearby saw the big dorsal fin, and pretty soon everyone saw the shark, too. Eli ran lickety split, making a huge splashing sound . . . just like all those folks who die in *Jaws*. Everyone knows that sharks are attracted to noise. And apparently everyone forgets. Clearly, Eli did. And there was our kid, with Shark-On-A-Stick. He ran away, all right. Only, he forgot to drop the stick.

Panic spread to every kid in the shallow water. John Philip Sousa never stood a chance keeping their attention after that. Fireworks were bursting, the music was playing, and Eli had a shark at stick's length. His parents, of course, were completely unaware.

Luckily, a local recognized the big catch for what it was, a sand shark. They are generally docile, but Eli the Shark Catcher was forever cemented in the minds of a hundred little kids that night. I'd bet they are still telling the tale.

Well, one of them is.

ooooo

Another big island year, we were swimming off Gay Head when Eli probably, really, almost definitely drowned. At least in the retelling.

Gay Head is arguably the most beautiful spot on the island. It's certainly one of the most dramatic. Gay Head is a long, curvy drive from the port towns, so it doesn't get very many day-trippers in for a snooze on the beach. It does, however, get plenty of surfers, which tells you a bit about the size of the waves. We were all bobbing in those waves with Eli and his friend Will, who had come with us from Vermont. As we were playing around, the waves began to get a bit stronger, so I headed to shore for a break.

The ocean turned inky, and a soft mist began to rise up around us. By the time I got to the shore, I realized that I could hardly make out John and the kids. We could all see each other just fine amongst the waves, but closer in to shore the clouds were hanging over the tops of the cliffs, while a fog was hazing everything on land.

Obviously a serious storm was coming in. I started to head back out and tell my people to come back in, but then I decided that they would have noticed the conditions and come in before I could get back out to them. So I sat on our quilt. And fretted.

I could have called out to them, but that would have been futile. The waves were loud on the best day, and with the storm . . . well, even I'm not that loud. Finally John came out of the water, laughing. Well, no worries then.

Only then he, too, noticed the storm. Apparently, it was still mostly invisible to the swimmers.

"So, did you leave our family out there?" I may have asked.

"Er, well, we were all having a good time. It was fun. I'm sure they'll be right behind me. Besides, the waves were fun-sized. Nothing scary at all."

John headed to the parking lot to get the car and agreed to meet us by the road as soon as everyone wandered up onshore. He didn't seem worried.

Fine. I didn't have to worry. I mean, I could no longer see the waves through the fog, and the kids didn't, in fact, come out right behind John, so I was totally fine. Or not. Okay, I panicked a little. I had officially lost *all* of my kids.[11]

So, on the beach alone with no husband and the kids missing, I wandered out to the edge of the water again. Maybe I should just swim out to them. Except, of course, now I couldn't see them at all. In fact, once I abandoned that notion, I realized that I couldn't find the quilt either. Well, shit.

I wandered around for a bit in the fog, when I heard the kids.

---

11. I do know that I just mentioned almost losing Eli on the Fourth of July while he swam with sharks, but really, I *am* a conscientious parent. I am. Often a couple of years in a row go by without my losing any of them. For long.

The laughing and yelling kids. Well, at least there was laughing.

I walked toward where I thought they were and eventually they came into view. Everyone was in one piece. No one had a shark on a stick—so I counted that a win. Eli, though, looked a little less sunny than the others. Well, as long as everyone was safe.

I bundled up our quilt and we made our way to John and the car. Everyone crashed inside—our own little wave—and the tale erupted out of Eli.

"I almost DROWNED!" For a near-death experience, he seemed pretty excited about it. "I got pulled under and couldn't get back up. It was a RIPTIDE! I almost DROWNED!"

"Eli, honey," Hannah calmly reassured, "you were under for about five seconds. Oh my God, Eli, we *all* went under." She turned to me. "The waves were fantastic, Mom. You went in too soon. It was just getting good."

Benjamin was thrilled with the whole enterprise. "I was getting air above those waves!"

Eli, though, was having none of this silliness. "I am telling you it was a RIPTIDE! I couldn't swim and my lungs burned from how long I had to hold my breath. I was upside down and I couldn't tell where the surface was. I couldn't tell up from down, and then I was SLAMMED down in this swirling hole of water. And then there was this powerful VICE of water. Yeah, it was like a TORNADO under there. I hit my head on something and then my leg on something else and then I think I threw my shoulder out from PUNCHING my way out!"[12]

He stopped to take a breath, his face contorted with drama and angst.

I was a little horrified.

Benjamin and Hannah were laughing. Will was clearly wonder-

---

12. He comes from a long line of overreactors.

ing if maybe Eli had really almost drowned out there.

Eli may be generally quiet like his dad but he has always loved a dramatic story.[13] His sentences are often punctuated with powerful burning and slashes and speeding thunderous tumbles. It is a little hard to know for sure when he has fallen off his skateboard or come crashing through a window into a pit of vipers. With machine guns.

It's funny how this tiny, quiet little New England beach can sound terrifying when Eli describes it.

ooooo

Of course, the island is special to all of us. Benjamin is the outdoorsman of the group. He and Steve had often found fishing to be one of their common languages. John could always speak Benjamin's language, but he would take the very young Benjamin fishing, too. They never caught anything, but Benjamin has more than made up for that in the years since. And Steve was always good for new equipment. When we started spending time on the island, Benjamin thought that he'd try shore fishing. He packed his Vermont fly rod and while we were all far out in the waves, he walked the shore casting his line.

He got the first tug while we were pretty far out, so we missed his excitement when he realized that he had hooked his first ocean fish. It didn't take long before we knew something was happening, though. Eli spotted some commotion on the shore and started trying to yell to us over the waves. Eventually he just pointed to the beach and I caught on.

A good-size crowd had gathered together, shielding their eyes from the sun and looking out into the water. My first thought was— Shark!

This is what happens when recently-city-people who know

---

13. Like his mom.

nothing at all about water wildlife come and stay too long at the beach trying to act like locals. I'd watched Shark Week, after all. And Eli had probably provoked them with that damned sand shark.

Well, shit.

Okay, what I did remember about sharks was that they mostly come out at dusk. Well, it wasn't dusk so that was no help. They are nearsighted! Yes, so, nearsighted, which means I'm supposed to just move out of their way when they come close. Right, casually step aside from the giant thing with teeth approaching from the murky depths. Got it.

Shit. Fuck. Shit.[14]

I started swimming to shore and scanning the water around me. And that's when I saw Benjamin. His pole was curled over and he was fighting the waves and the rod—half-swimming, half-walking. It was apparently a big fish. Looking back at the crowd I could see they were all following along with my boy as he fought whatever was on the end of that line.

So, not a shark.

It was just my kid with a big fish.

Right.

Unless, of course, the shark was on the end of his line. At which point, Eli called out, "That's my brother!" So I guess he thought it might have been a shark, too. My boys and their sharks.

We made it to the beach and Eli went for the camera. He was working the crowd and drumming up support for his big brother. I worked my way in closer to our young Hemingway as he was chest-deep in salt water, rod curled over, arms straining above his head. I got in close enough to be heard and called out, "Oh, Benjamin.

---

14. Some situations demand a stronger response. Being in an unrehearsed *Jaws* remake was apparently one of those.

Look, honey, the whole beach is watching!"

He didn't respond, but did sort of look in my direction. I guess he couldn't hear me. So I pointed at the shore—like Eli had.

He followed along the line of sight of my finger and saw the crowd gathered as the rod took another dip and turn, struggling to slip out of his hands.

He said, "Oh ju—Fu, marunch the bec I AM farunling to hoffer!!"

Well then.

I couldn't make out the words, but I did get the gist of it. The news alert from his proudly smiling mom had not been welcome. He had an audience. A big audience. He also had a flimsy, Vermont-mountain-stream fly rod, light line, and all the testosterone and ego that a young man could muster. So, now he *had* to land this fish. Before, it could have been the one that got away. Now he was going to have to actually win this particular fight. Sorry, honey.

He was all grim determination at that point. He came in closer to shore and then wandered down the beach into the higher, pounding water. For more than half an hour his arms were straining and that line jigged and joggled, while he tried to outlast whatever fish . . . shark . . . submarine . . . whatever, he had hooked. Over half an hour of grunting and hauling and a little bit of prayer I didn't know he had in him. But eventually, painstakingly, he hauled a striped bass out of the waters off Martha's Vineyard. Fifty inches long and shining.

Eli helped him wrap it in a towel before he slung it over his shoulder and marched triumphantly through the crowd.

We were going to be having sushi for supper.

The next year we had to figure out how to pack the "good" fishing gear into the cars. I think we wrapped it in scarves and hid a few candles in the tackle box.

○○○○○

MAKING HOME

The table moves around when home does.

One of the first things we bought Benjamin when he moved out, and Hannah, when she did, too, was a good table. Benjamin's, like his personality, is a contemporary red metal with a high shine. There is an industrial feel to it. In his house, mixed in with a few quirky antiques, it is a bright enigma. It is where he edits his movies and where the grouse and trout he's brought home are served for dinner.

Hannah and Dan had a tiny little Manhattan space when they moved in together, so their antique walnut table sits snugly in one corner. It has leaves that can widen it or make it smaller as events dictate. This is where the vegetarian creativity gets served and where Dan does homework for the MBA he is working on by night. There are often flowers and almost always candles glowing there.

The table is the heart of a home.

On island, there is the big gray picnic table on the deck where morning coffee with the loons singing in the background helps us start the day. Inside, there is a less-than-thrilling plain modern maple table. It is the place we gather in the evening after long sun-drenched days on the beach or days spent playing dress-up in Edgartown, fundraising for the client.

One of us stops by a farmers' market and lugs home corn and tomatoes most days. We basket-shop on island. Grocery stores are only for coffee, milk, butter, and pasta. The rest we grab at local farmstands. We cart and carry good balsamics and olives from Vermont, so when we are on island a shoulder basket can hold the fruits and vegetables, maybe a loaf of homemade bread for another good panzanella salad. There is always fresh false albacore or striper at the fish market, which John grills and I crumble in amongst the greens, tomatoes, and crispy hunks of grilled bread turned into clunky croutons soaking up the balsamic.

And this functional table becomes lovely when laden with bowls of steaming pasta and fish, mismatched candles of every shape and size, and always, always a bunch of bright roadside flowers right in the middle. We come together once or twice most every day. Sometimes it is in the rush of coffee and croissants. Sometimes it is over a long dinner that gets cooked and eaten in fits and starts.

We might make a salad and then go for a swim before the sun sets on the pond. That means everyone will have to pitch in, peeling the beets and shaving the cheese for the main course, which often won't get served much before ten. Then we check our watches to see if there is time to run down to the ice-cream parlor and back. We are, with lightning bugs and dogs at our feet, back around the picnic table as the evening cools and talk turns to the novels we are reading or a late-night movie. Can we all stand to watch *Jaws* one more time? These are not the tables we would choose in a store, and yet they are as much a part of the fabric of our lives as any of the ones that we have handpicked.

One year there was a fight about a fish caught and not thrown back. Guests were treated to sullen, animal-loving recriminations, and a loud, proud fisherman overboasting. But come morning, the dogs needed walking and the coffee was brewing. There was bacon and local farm eggs. And eventually there were reluctant hugs, as we all moved passed it. None of us really changed our minds or positions, but we all scooted over and made room for the dissension and disappointment. It comes with the territory, and whenever someone else shows up for dinner, even when the guest is just a bad mood, we make room. Luckily the table is usually big enough.

CHAPTER FIVE

Imperfect

THE SUMMER HAD TAKEN A TOLL. WE HAD BEEN BACK FOR almost two whole months and we still weren't getting much done. For one thing, we really needed to put the garden to bed. Old dead vines, once filled with zucchini and tomatoes, looked downtrodden and messy in the middle of all this coming autumnal wonder. It was almost October, and their day was past. It seemed almost mean to leave them looking so miserable.

Plus, Steve was coming for a visit the next weekend. And I always like the house and yard to shine when we have guests. The coming weekend promised sunshine and temperatures in the sixties: perfect weather for putting the garden to bed. We were going to whip this family back in shape.

The cool sunshine was also perfect for a thin sweater, long skirt, and cowboy boots. Sometimes you just gotta dress for the tourists. They think we all look like this every day. Little do they know that by the middle of stick season, deep into November, when the winds are howling and the trees bare, we run to the grocery store in six layers including an old flannel nightgown whose torn edges are flapping around good Canadian boots. From November until April, the boots and the lip balm are the only designer affectations we can abide. But in September, we romanticize and dress the part in old Black Watch vests over burnt-orange sweaters next to the boots and long skirts that look like an ad for the Sundance catalog.

Unfortunately, nothing in the outfit seemed right for putting away the garden. So we decided to take a drive instead.

This is a great time of year for going for a ride in the car. The leaves are just turning, and every Vermont town is getting ready for the tourists. You can stop in one after another of the little villages to find trucks selling cider and cheese along the sides of the road. There are craft fairs around every bend, and the mountains are in their early-Autumn Sunday best. John and I got so carried away that we made our way into a wine shop in Ludlow. We not only bought wine, but a corkscrew and real glasses. All the better to look the part. We found a sweet spot on Mount Tom, where we sipped wine, held hands, and felt grateful. September was a big part of why we'd moved here, after all. This was the time of year that made people cash in their savings, uproot their children, and come to the glorious beauty that is a Vermont autumn.

The next morning was just as sunny, and the garden was, of course, still just as sad. So after a big breakfast, we decided that this would be the day. The leaves were piling up, like the snowdrifts would in a few weeks.

"John, we should really do something about those leaves while we're working on the garden. We should at least make a dent in them," I suggested.

John said, "Look up."

I looked at the millions of leaves in the hundred or so trees around the house.

"Okay. But we should rake for the same reason that we make the bed."

John grinned and headed out to the garden. I opened up the basement and hauled out the garden tools. But then I heard him calling me from up on the hill above the garden, which is ringed by old maples. He'd spread a soft quilt on the ground and suggested that we should maybe lie down to watch the leaves fall.

And so that's what we did. We lay under those trees and watched the leaves drift. The garden could wait.

Surrounded on that little hill by more than a dozen maples that have been growing there for most of a century, we watched as leaves floated quietly down, twirled and spun in an early hurrah of the ancient red-and-orange hula.

Minutes turned into hours. Before long, the morning was gone. The farmers' market was closing at two, so we ran off for cheese, apples, and salty bread stuffed with kale and garlic.

We did get back to the garden. Eventually. The plants were cut back, and the bright-red tomato cages were tucked away in six-foot rows, waiting for spring. By late afternoon, the cool sunshine had faded to a chilly evening, so we carried wood up from the basement and filled the wood closet. Just in case.

The next day dawned sunny and mild. We tramped back outside with coffee and quilt before work. Time for another round of leaf peeping. At this rate, we figured we would actually bear witness to the falling of the leaves even if we didn't manage to tuck the garden in. But you can't do everything. In most years, this leaf show blows away in one drama queen of a windstorm. But this year it was ever so gently moving along. And this year, especially this year, I decided not only to look out over these mountains and admire the views that roll down our way, but to look up instead of down. The symbolism is not lost on me.

I found myself focusing on an insistent internal dialogue . . . a reminder. The gray years of the Horrible Quaint Country Store had faded. We had gotten another beginning here. So, in this gentle fall with this man I have loved for so long, I would gratefully remember to always look up. Because, this place is the most beautiful spot on earth for two or three weeks out of the year.[1] I would bear witness to the falling of these leaves, and I would feel glad and full and not worry

---

1. The rest of the time it is merely *one* of the most beautiful.

about the winter. Winter always comes, but here in this high valley amid these old mountains, I am reminded that the gaudy Technicolor always comes back. We just have to remember to watch the show.

○○○○○

Okay, I do have a garden, so that's a plus. But the thing is, I am just going to say this . . . I don't recycle.

There, I've said it.

Out loud.

I do feel guilty about it.

I mean, when you are raising children you want them to be responsible world citizens. You want them to contribute to their communities and add more than they take. And you are the main example to them. It is the parent's job to teach them how to live these value-filled lives. Plus, if you have up and moved your entire family to the People's Republic of Vermont, where lefty liberal values are served at breakfast with a heaping side of granola, you also don't want to have your face on a poster in the local post office.

But it's the truth.

I don't recycle.

Every year at Christmas when all those catalogs come in the mail, I toy with the idea of buying some really attractive, eco-friendly recycling bins for our mudroom. Smith & Hawken had some cool wooden ones a while back. Restoration Hardware had something that looked like it might work, too. Once, I even ordered some bins from a yuppie lifestyle place.

The delivery guy pulled up to our house and I was, initially, excited. Everyone likes a delivery. But then he started unloading the boxes. He was carrying them off the truck, awkwardly struggling under them. They were just so huge. I looked at the delivery guy, and then I turned and looked at my little mudroom. I thought, and I'm not proud of this, *Where will we put our shoes?*

A green planet, or a spot to stow our shoes? Hmm.

I mean, it's a question of practicality here. Besides, how will the dogs have a place to shake if we give up all the space to old orange-juice containers? We can't add a trash room onto the house in addition to a mudroom. This house predates the Lincoln administration. There must certainly be rules about that.

The UPS guy hobbled up to the door with a "Delivery for Stimson?"

I got a whiff of the future smells that would greet me when I came in over the threshold. Not that the UPS guy smelled. I'm sure he didn't. I mean metaphorical . . . precognitive smells. I imagined a hint of spoiled milk like when the kids were babies and every single piece of clothing I owned had the perfume of old milk on it. A rough smell, but in the end they grew up and now I've got these kids who hardly ever smell like spoiled anything.

I imagined a cocktail of peanut butter and orange juice wafting up on a warm summer morning. I considered giving up milk. Peanut butter. Orange juice. And then a noxious intuition of all three hit me at once and I gagged. Yes, I actually gagged right there in my driveway, in all that sweet mountain air.[2]

UPS Guy looked a little taken aback. I looked a little green.

I refused the shipment. Of course I did.

So, UPS Guy struggled those ridiculous bins back into his truck. Muttering, I'm certain. And I went inside, skulking around like I'd set a forest fire maybe. Smokey the Bear stood in the corner, shaking his head at me. I felt vaguely like a 1970s litterbug who had somehow time-traveled to the twenty-first century. They were going to put me in a stockade.

In the end, I forgave myself. Well, someone had to.

---

2. I have a very clear and vivid imagination.

I even started researching the costs and energy required to recycle. After a while, I began thinking that the benefits of recycling were probably overstated after all. Recycling is a manufacturing process. The question of whether it uses less or more energy than primary manufacturing varies. So okay, I may have been giving my kids mixed messages about the planet, but I was at least encouraging critical thinking. That has to count for something. I hoped.

The reality was that the issue was for me about space.

And the smells.

Okay, it was really really about the smells.

And . . . look, I just don't recycle.

It still comes up, of course. All. The. Time.

We frequently have guests come to stay with us. Some guests are friends from the island. Sarah and Aaron, good, responsible citizens. Some are friends from our old lives back in St. Louis where we all taught our kids together about the planet and our role as its stewards. And, of course, my dear friend Patricia from Manhattan. Of course, she recycles. Of course she does. They all look askance the first time they ask where they should put the can, plastic container . . . whatever . . . and I say, maybe a little challengingly, "The trash."

It is an imperfect answer.

But they give in. I'm the host. It's my house. And they are gracious guests. So, to the trash it goes. Time goes by, many visits later in most cases, and they will walk through the house with a juice-thingy[3] in their hands and pause for just a second as if suddenly remembering something. I have seen this particular pause a thousand times now. It just freezes them there. It's the Did-I-Leave-The-Oven-On pause. The Where-Did-I-Put-My-Keys pause. Or in this case the Where-Is-The-Recycling-Bin-Oh-Yeah-This-Is-Ellen's-House pause.

---

3. It's the technical term.

And then, the ones who love me seem to sort of shake it off[4] and they toss the thingy in the trashcan.

The others don't get invited back.

Hell with 'em.

It's not like I smoke cigarettes. Or beat my kids. Or wander the woods of the 1970s starting forest fires. Smokey can have a seat.

I just don't want to have to rinse out smelly things and then leave them hanging around in my small mudroom until next Thursday. I mean, blech.

Of course, sometimes a well-meaning person will try and help me.

This is a strategy that always works.

Like suggesting that maybe I'd want to skip dessert after the holidays. Or suggesting that maybe if I gave up coffee I'd be a little less likely to bark at them when they mentioned dessert.

Anyway, a well-meaning person generally mentions "the planet" . . . like maybe I have been on another one for the last ten years and hadn't heard about climate change or finite resources or how long plastic lives. I tend to sneer. It's a nice sneer. I've practiced it. This usually neatly ends the whole thing.

I mean, come on. I had kids. I watched all the kid television. I know about the planet . . . the climate . . . the finite resources . . . plastic. I just do not like bad smells!

This is the point where a few guests decide that now is the time to explain just how easy the whole process is.

"You see, Ellen. All you have to do is . . ."

Maybe I am just a little slow. I mean, it's clear I don't know how use a knife and fork properly. Maybe I just need a little lesson in this easy new thing the kids are doing: Recycling!

---

4. When in Rome. Or Dorset.

So then I throw my own politics up against theirs. I figure that yes, I'm the host, but they started it.

"You know, I have chickens. What exactly do you do with your garbage and leftover food?"

Okay, so some do reply, "Compost," but most, thankfully, do not. I can end the debate right there. I get to hold my head up.

"Look, I feed the girls my garbage, they fertilize my garden, and then they give me eggs. It's a nice little arrangement that feeds my home and reduces waste going into a landfill. We each do our part in our own way."

See. I've seen the commercials. I'm doing my bit for the planet. I'm socially conscious. So there.

Okay, so the reality is that I do not give a shit about this particular issue. I care about a lot of issues. This one just isn't mine. The way I see it, you can't save every starfish on the beach.

I am plenty political. I give money to ethical candidates. I write articles and letters. I help get out the vote. I have issues that I focus on intensely, and work hard to help solve.

Just not this one.

I try not to ask the self-righteous recyclers what they are doing about world hunger. When they are women, I fantasize about asking them how they feel about the little girls in Afghanistan. And don't get me started on our own cultural misogyny.

At this point the mental haranguing starts in.

Do you write checks to EMILY's List? Do you make phone calls for women candidates? When I really get going I've been known to use my outside voice. Well, I was willing to let it lie at the chickens. They kept me going.

Usually, though, the conversation is just with a passing dinner guest who won't be back. Really. They won't be back.

Anyway, most miss my point, anyway. The truth is that all of us are doing our part to stop some horrible problem. And we are, also, equally neglecting our duty somewhere else. Like I said, you can't save every starfish on the beach. You do what you can.

And if you don't pick recycling, and especially if you live in Vermont, I can tell you this: You will be judged.

Often.

ooooo

Hannah recycles. She has since she was little. And she has a few tiny little opinions on the subject.

To complicate matters, she is not just an occasional guest. She lived with us. As you might imagine. So I guess that makes her one of the regulars.

One day I noticed this really terrible smell.

Well, I know that things spill. I've got three kids. But it was a nasty smell. So I took steps. I cleaned out the refrigerator. I emptied everything out and scrubbed. Hands-and-knees scrubbed.

I stood back, surveyed my work proudly and . . . I smelled it. Still there.

Okay. It wasn't the fridge.

So I took the trashcan outside. I hosed it down with bleach and water. There was more scrubbing. I sniffed at the trashcan. I looked closely. It was ready. So I brought it back into the kitchen. Put in a fresh liner.

And, of course, no better. There was still that . . . smell.

That left the cabinets. I started opening drawers and doors looking for a source. Anything. Something had to be causing this. I hoped it wasn't anything dead. Or worse, alive.

I was about four cabinets into the search[5] when I found her stash. There's a hidden cupboard to the side of the stove, where we

---

5. Did I mention that hands and knees were involved here, again? This wasn't a cursory glance.

keep the seldom-used appliances. Tucked up next to the food processor was a pile of (mostly) empty containers. Smelly containers. I wanted to throttle her.

Apparently, Hannah had been cursorily washing these things. Very cursorily, if you ask me. And then hiding them till trash day. Of course, trash day would come and she wouldn't remember until it was too late. But that was okay, she'd just remember next week. Judging by the pile, this had been going on for months. Months! Trash day came early that week.

Naturally, it isn't just the recycling with Hannah. She's a twenty-first-century girl. She also hates plastic bags from the store. Well, me too. We have a point of agreement. It's nice to be on the side of the righteous. I have a bunch of lovely cloth bags that I use. We keep Cronig's bags from the Vineyard. And Dorset Farmers Market ones, too. We have some funky totes that our favorite young friend Michelle Krasny makes at her environmentally hip company, Nestle-berry.[6] I even have a whole bunch of flowery bags that we used to carry at Peltier's.[7]

Only, there's the trouble. I mean, you use these wonderful cloth bags for your groceries and you're feeling smug for the rest of the day. You can carry the groceries in, and save the world from all those leftover plastic bags. Then you hang them in your mud-room, which is just big enough for the bags, but far too small for the recycling bins that you refused delivery on. Well, that's what I do. I intend to take them back out to the car so that I'll have them the next time I stop at the store. Only, I never do.

Which means that the next time I go to the grocery store, I have to buy more cloth bags. Okay, so it's not perfect. But still, these

---

6. We have a deal: I buy her products, and she doesn't chastise me. I love her.

7. Lots of these. Want some?

bags are really useful, and what's a few more. It'll just mean that we can have some at home and some in the car. What's the problem?

The problem is that I did that for . . . let's just call it a long time . . . and now I have this *enormous* collection of bags. Eventually I just gave in under the mountain of cloth bags blocking my way through the mudroom, and went back to the plastic. Apparently, my mudroom has it out for the planet.

Hannah, of course, was upset about the plastic bags. Rather than trying to modify my behavior, though, she thought we should, at least minimally, reuse them. Sure, all these terrible little bags will end up in a landfill at some point, but until then she wanted to make sure we had a couple of uses with them. Conscientious, our Hannah.

At one point, we must have had . . . oh, a thousand . . . of those things rattling around in every drawer, cabinet, and closet in the house. She would stash them, and I would ignore it . . . for a while. But eventually I would just throw away her stash. I just had to. They were everywhere, and she wasn't really using them. We were a plastics retirement home. It was becoming a problem. So she would stash the plastic bags in a different drawer or cabinet. Then I would come across the stash and throw it out. And she'd move to a new stash. It was a game of liar's poker.

In late September during her senior year, Hannah had come home for the weekend from Mount Holyoke. Steve was visiting for a little fly-fishing with Benjamin, so she had come back home to visit, too. We were all talking about spring, when she would graduate from college. Steve was planning to come back for that as well. I reminded him that bourbon was a liquid. He mentioned how nice the Jacuzzi would be for that week. The trouble was that there was this tiny little problem with graduation.

The problem was that Mount Holyoke only gave each of their young women four tickets.

Four.

John, Benjamin, Eli, and me.

They had, maybe thoughtlessly, overlooked the ticket category of Former Husbands Who Are Part of the Package. Also, Far-Flung Grandmothers Who Absolutely Need to See Their Favorite Grandchild Graduate.

Everybody has favorites. Some of us hide it better than others. John's mother, Dorothy, had just stopped trying. Dorothy had grown up with girls. She had three sisters. Then, in her grown-up life, she'd raised five boys. Five boys. So, our Hannah, this special granddaughter, was the first girl of Dorothy's own. She was forever and truly bonded. Four plus two. So, we needed six.

Steve offered up a solution.

"Look, I'll break Dorothy in. What'll they do? Kick out a grandmother? Besides, if we can't make it in, I'll take her to a bar and we'll just watch the ceremony on the local TV station."

"Or get arrested," someone offered.

"Arrested? No way. I've got a way with these situations. It'll be fine." Steve seemed pretty sure of himself.

We strictly forbade trying to smuggle any of his home distillery's finest in with Dorothy. His criminal record probably couldn't take it. And I'm not sure she would be up for fingerprinting and mug shots while he explained that it was just a small little bottle after all.

It was a happy, meandering conversation about stolen seats and minor crimes. Only then I heard, "Hey, Mom? Where are the bags?" Hannah was apparently on eco-patrol.

"Bags?" I innocently asked.

"*Mo-mmm?!!*"[8]

It had been such a nice morning.

---

8. Two syllables. Two exclamation points.

"I don't know, sweetie. Which bags are you talking about?" I figured that ignorance was the best first defense.

Steve was sitting at the kitchen table. John was making a cappuccino, and I was at the stove. Hannie was in the middle of the triangle.

"*Da-ad*." She pivoted to the second parent for support.

"What?" Because even John knew that ignorance was the place to start.

"You know perfectly well what. I have been gone for three weeks, and you let her throw away all those bags." In the face of ignorance, it seemed that Hannah had gone with the reasonable-explanation-of-the-facts move. Fine. I could handle that. Steve, however, was a bit off-balance. He didn't see that he was involved in the crime. By association or proximity, he was the third parent-like adult in the room.

"Bags?" Well, he was curious what the fuss was about.

"Ohmygod Steve, do *you* recycle?!" Hannah didn't seem to know whether she'd just discovered another earth-hating landfill glutton or a comrade-in-arms. A good "Ohmygod" would straighten it out.

"Sure I do," he replied.

Oh great.

We were all going to drown in the storm of indignation. Of course, I didn't believe him for a minute. He lived a thousand miles away. She couldn't check. He knew it. But I knew him. So I figured I'd set the record straight.

"You do not," I said. "Come on. Since when?" I might have been a little accusatory.

"Since just now when Hannah asked me." He laughed it off, but wanted to maintain that he, too, was on the righteous recycling side. "I'm only kidding. I have a blue bin that the city picks up once a week. I throw things in there. So, yes, I recycle." Well, that launched her well and truly.

"Mom, *everybody* recycles. Except you and Dad. And Daddy *would* recycle, only you throw everything away before he gets a chance."

John had just about gotten a perfect head of foam on his cappuccino. He was using the time to look across the kitchen minefield. He was clearly wondering how he could tiptoe through and make his escape.

"Dad, you promised you would at least keep the bags." Caught between espresso, a wife, and a daughter. John looked to Steve and saw no help there. Well. He seemed to think playing for time and playing the befuddled dad would at least help.

"Oh, you mean the grocery bags?" As if he'd just discovered these people in his kitchen and was slowly catching up to their conversation. He shifted his grip on the cappuccino at that point. "They have a big bin at Shaw's now. You can leave your bags there to be recycled."

Stick to simple, declarative statements. Just the facts. It was a good plan. Hannah, though, had the advantage of having met her father.

"Ohhh, really? And did you take the bags there, then?"

He stuck to his guns: Push onward. That's a good plan, right. So he replied that "The bin is right by their front door. And it's really tall. It holds a lot. They could even handle our hundred and sixty-seven."

"We had a hundred and sixty-seven?" John's specificity gave her pause. Good move.

"Well, something like that. We had a lot."

Relieved and still more than a little righteous, Hannah answered, "Finally, there is a little sanity in this house."

I stirred the cheddar grits. Hannah grabbed a cloth bag and headed out to clean her car.

Steve looked up and said, "John, I listened closely. I did not hear you actually say that you took the bags to be recycled."

John blew on his foam.

"What bags, Steve?"

It takes a village.[9]

ooooo

Eli had been back in regular school for a couple of years at this point. I missed homeschooling him, but he had lobbied for a while for the bustle of a kid-filled school. So in seventh grade, he had gone back. We had all adapted.

Eli thought school was a place for lots of playing, and for planning for later play. School was filled with kids. What else could it possibly be there for if not for lots of play? If Eli couldn't kick it, throw it, or eat it, he didn't want it.

But then, this year had turned hard. Many of his friends left Long Trail after eighth grade for Manchester's high school. Vermont has an ancient voucher system where you can take your town's school allowance to any high school. Our little village of Dorset was blessed with a high tax base and our residents got a higher allowance than the state average. We could take that money to the local private school, where it covered a bunch of the tuition, or we could take it to Manchester, where it covered everything.

Each year at Town Meeting, Dorset voted to match the school allowance to the tuition of the high school, Burr and Burton Acad-

---

9. Writing about this has kicked up the guilt factor. Even Benjamin, who just read this, said, "Mom, I don't think you can tell this. Really, you ought to just do it. It's not that hard." I guess I'll go look at Restoration Hardware. Maybe it's time.

emy in Manchester. Several other "sending" towns, that is, towns without their own high schools, did this, too. So, BBA was essentially free to families who lived in Dorset. That meant that many families chose to commute after eighth grade. BBA is a top-rated semiprivate school, so in ninth grade it attracted lots of our region's best and brightest.

Eli wanted to go. All his friends were going. So what if the classes were bigger? They weren't all that much bigger. It was an incredibly well-funded school. Yes, he knew we preferred a divergent education model, but this was his education we were talking about, not ours. A fair point.

And besides, his best friend Timmy was going to BBA. Eli and Timmy had been best friends throughout our homeschooling years when Timmy went to the local elementary school. Through middle school, Timmy went to Dorset's middle school and Eli went to Long Trail. Eli was excited about finally sharing a classroom with his best bud. It had been a point of discussion and dissension throughout the previous spring. In our family, the parents take on as much debate and discussion as the kids want on the big stuff, but we reserve the right to make the decisions. The underlying theory is that somebody has to eventually make the decisions, and we have the broadest view, the most experience making decisions, a strategic value model, and we always have the best interests of the family as our guiding principle.

That, anyway, is the theory.

So Eli was going back to Long Trail in the fall for ninth grade despite his best arguments. We wanted him to try its high school. We did, however, agree that if after a year he was still unhappy, we would reconsider. Happiness and life satisfaction, after all, are parts of the strategic model.

Only, over the summer on the island, Eli had gotten sick. Sick for real. And the trip had turned dark. It was the kind of sick that changes things. We had some old friends from St. Louis visiting just for the day. They had been vacationing over on the Cape and we planned a day showing them Martha's Vineyard for their first time. They had two little girls, so we started on the carousel in Oak Bluffs when they got off the boat. We followed that with breakfast at Art Cliff in Vineyard Haven, which offers up the best breakfasts I have ever eaten anywhere.[10] Eli wasn't feeling well and decided to go back to the house while we headed for the pond. He would catch up to us that night for lobster and the sunset at Menemsha.

We stopped by the house later on, and he still had a headache and fever. We left him comfortable, and went on without him. This was a teenager who could presumably stay under the covers with the remote, getting himself toast for a few hours, while we entertained these people we had not seen in five years.

We got home late that night, and Eli was asleep. I felt his forehead, and it was still kind of warm. So I got him some water and Motrin before I woke him up. He said he was achy.

We had had a lot of big summer fun this trip. I guessed that he was just run down, and had gotten a virus. It wasn't kicking up his asthma, so I wasn't too worried. That, like so many other assumptions and predictions we would make over the next few days, turned out to be wrong.

By the third day, I was calling around looking for island doctors who would see a tourist patient. His fever wasn't high, but it was constant. I was beginning to worry. I found a local doc who could

---

10. I have dedicated many hours to testing this principle. Art Cliff Diner wins every time. Their lemon crepes are perfect and the goodness of the lobster Benedict cannot be overstated. The crabby hash has its fans too. Art Cliff. Not to be missed. Call us. We'll take you.

see us that morning. Eli's aches had escalated, and just walking hurt his whole body. His head was pounding. I started worrying about the big stuff, like meningitis. I must have asked him fifty times to put his chin to his chest while we drove to the doctor's office.

While we were waiting to be seen, he fell asleep. That was weird. By the time they called us, he could barely stand up. He rallied in the examining room, but the doctor got the vibe immediately. He sent us straight to the emergency room for blood work.

Eli's speech began to slur within a couple of hours as we waited for the blood work. By five o'clock that afternoon, his temperature was 105. He was no longer cogent. He couldn't even hold his head up. We were way past scared.

When the tests came back, we found out that it wasn't meningitis. It was, instead, a virulent reaction to Lyme disease and babisiosis, which is not unlike malaria only usually far less severe. Rarely, people have toxic reactions to these two. Eli was one of those people. It turns out that there is a terrible tick problem on the island. There is, even, a renowned tick lab at the hospital in Falmouth, Massachusetts. So Eli was in the right place for a fast and accurate diagnosis.

After a few days of antibiotics, he was just "normal serious sick" rather than "terrifying sick." We got an air-conditioned hotel room to help us manage the fevers. The fevers were lower now, but constant.[11] Our little house was breezy and perfect for sleeping after happy days at the beach. It was less perfect for managing serious illness. And our boy was too weak for a long trip involving boats and cars. Going home seemed riskier than holing up here for a while.

We were in touch with our regular doctors back in Vermont and pediatric specialists in Boston. John stayed at the house with the

---

11. They would recur for months afterwards.

dogs and came back and forth to the hotel. We got piles of books, and Eli let me read to him again just like when he was little. Sometimes in the afternoons, we would sit on the balcony and watch the seagulls. Mostly, though, we stayed in the air conditioning.

It was freezing in there, and I stayed bundled up in sweaters and shawls. We discovered a silly spy show called *Covert Affairs* that was marathoning the whole previous season, prior to the new season. We gorged on that and DVDs. Hannah, who was nannying on the island that summer, stopped by every day, even though we were some thirty minutes away. Most days she came twice. Benjamin came back to the island for a couple of long weekends just to visit his brother. He walked to Espresso Love and brought Eli the iced chai lattes made with heavy cream that he was living on. All the servers at Espresso Love were in on the treatment plan. These lattes were the only thing that tasted good to our patient, so they started making them with heavy cream to get some calories into him. Steve called every couple of days to check in. Aunt Mindy, Steve's sister, was calling, too.

This illness had been its own special kind of scary. Scary in the sitting-in-an-emergency-room-with-your-child-who-has-lost-the-ability-to-communicate kind of way. Parents who have done this are in a special club. I can tell you that it is a club you don't want to join and it takes a toll.

Months of antibiotics, and many difficult secondary infections later, Eli was well again. Skinny, but well. He lost a little over 20 percent of his body weight. And he had been skinny to begin with. It had been a long road. And it wasn't over.

ooooo

Benjamin had moved into this cute house in Pawlet, Vermont. He'd just completed the move and had a brand-new phone number to go with his brand-new life. Eli couldn't remember the number. Benjamin had moved in three months before, but Eli just couldn't seem to learn it.

"What's Benjamin's phone number again?" he asked. Again.

"It's on the bulletin board in the kitchen, remember? What, do you have teenage Alzheimer's or something?" I laughed.

Then I stopped laughing. I looked at him. He'd asked me for that number at least twenty times. I realized that, all joking aside, something was wrong.

"What?" he tossed off after looking at the number as he headed into the library. The library is about twenty steps from the kitchen bulletin board.

As soon as he got to the phone he called out, "What's that number again?" He sounded a little frustrated.

I walked in and looked at him. I told him the number. He held my gaze.

He said, "I can't remember it."

"I know," I replied. "You were really sick, sweetie. Maybe it's something with that. Don't worry about it. We'll figure it out."

But he did worry. And so did John. So did I.

He was in ninth grade and taking high school physics. And he couldn't remember the formulas. None of them.

We knew we had a problem.

ooooo

November was tough that year. Then Zoë died.

It just kept coming.

Zoë was Eli's Bengal cat. When he was seven and we were homeschooling, Eli had wanted a kitten for Christmas. The idea of writing a school report on cats sprang from that Christmas wish. He researched all kinds of breeds and discovered Bengals, which he assured us were perfect pets for seven-year-old boys. And the light-colored ones were mostly hypoallergenic. They were smart, mischievous, and could be taught to fetch. Sort of like dogs in a cat suit. But, you know, still cats. And apparently they were big talkers. Every website said that. Big talkers? I wondered exactly what that meant.

Turned out that Eli was right. Zoë was a perfect fit for our family.

Bengals are shrunk cats. They are a mixture of domestic short-hair and Asian Leopard cat. There are layers of designations, and our little Zoë was an F6, which means six times removed from the original mating. These are not lap cats. They are curious and highly active. Their spotted coat looks remarkably like a leopard's. Zoë was a perfect example of the breed.

Zoë and Eli would play hide-and-seek in the yard for hours. When we walked with our dogs in the woods, she would walk right along, hopping across tree trunks and running up a tree every few hundred yards to impress the dogs. During the day, she played with three fox babies while the mama fox lounged in the sun. They would run big circles around the yard and she picked up a howling sound from them. She practiced it for hours. It was a haunting howl that made us run to the porch every single time. She would glance our way as if to say, "What? Umm, playing here."

She slept in Eli's bed every night. When I would go in to wake him up in the morning she would stick her head out of the covers near his and meow a good morning. She greeted everyone. She was chatty.

But then a horrible thing happened, when Eli was dealing with the memory problems. She had a stroke and died barely an hour later.

It was as simple and as devastating as that. She had been barely middle-aged, but still. Our only other cats, Sophie and Molly, had both lived to be eighteen. That had been the plan here, too. Only no one had told Zoë.

When Eli got home from school and we told him, I thought he would faint. All the color drained out of his body. He sagged and seemed almost to crumble into himself. We hugged and cried and held one another.

But only for a few days.

He just couldn't bear to talk about her at all. Benjamin and Hannah had each visited and tried to offer support right after it happened. They came, and as soon as they would start to tell a sweet Zoë story Eli would flee. They each asked us what they should do. Unfortunately, we didn't know either.

As days turned into weeks and weeks turned into months, it became clear that Eli had been wrecked by Zoë's loss. I would find him late at night alone by her grave. Grief is especially tough on teenage boys, I think. Their other teenage boy friends don't know how to help them process it, other than just kicking a ball really hard. They might allow that the situation sucks.

Though, come to think of it, maybe they are the real grief experts. Because it *is* really sad. And you *are* gong to be sad for a while. Eventually you will be less sad, but meanwhile it sucks. That about sums up the whole grief process, doesn't it?

Anyway, there is also this deep biological desire to be masculine and tough at that age. Feelings get buried or hidden behind something else. I think a lot of teenaged pot-smoking boys are just really, really sad about something. That was not an answer we wanted him to find. And we were starting to worry. He couldn't really talk about the loss at all. We are serious animal-people. The loss of a beloved pet hits us hard. But the rest of us weren't dealing with the all-around "suck" that Eli was.

We started lobbying for another kitty. It seemed like a solution. Eli wouldn't even consider it. We tried to give him time, but the signs weren't good. By Thanksgiving, we issued a decree. He had to pick something to get busy with and sidetrack his sad, racing mind. Soccer season was over, and the kid needed a diversion bad. School was a mess. Zoë was gone. It was a lot of sad. But it was a trap that we needed him to break out of.

He swore he did not want another kitten. So, fine, we put him to work on the problem.

I started out getting his attention. "Listen, kid. We love you." Best to establish that right up front. "But you are too sad. You are aiming for depression. We are sad, too, but we do not honor Zoë by closing up and not living. We honor those we love with our lives. Life is a gift. You can't stop using it, and we want to get you back in here."

At that age . . . well, hell, at any age . . . it's easy to get trapped in a sad cycle. Zoë's death was serious and sad, sure. But doing the same things every day. Walking the same mental circles. Well, that wasn't getting Eli through this. So we knew that a change needed to happen. I told him to make it a project.

"So we want you to do a little research and choose something new to do, buddyroe. You can take guitar or piano lessons. You can learn to fish with your brother. You can take a photography class at the college. But you need to get busy. I mean it. You have to choose something that will require your attention with lessons or practice five times per week."

He was wallowing. The sadness had seeped into him completely, and we knew that what he needed was a focus . . . something to pull him out of this funk.

"And meanwhile, you are going to yoga with Dad."

"Yoga?"

Though Eli felt like that was coming out of left field, it got his attention. It had been John's idea. He figured that Eli couldn't express his feelings, but obviously they were causing him pain. Maybe we could get at them through the body.

John had put it to me that "Teenage boys live totally in the physical world. Maybe if he goes to yoga with me, he can feel sad while realizing that he can feel other things, too. Right now, he is on the all-sad channel all the time." It was a thought. A pretty good one.

"Plus, I am in a hard part of the yoga practice. It will take all his concentration to keep up."

I married a smart guy.

And a loving one.

We had this.

Of course, Eli didn't want to go to yoga.

So we told him, "Six months. Give it a try. We are older. We know stuff. Trust us and give it a try."

And bless him. He did.

Naturally, this sweet father-son business ruined yoga for John. The teacher, a woman we all lovingly refer to as John's maharishi, amped up the classes to engage Eli. John could barely walk. But Eli? Eli was getting better.

John had a theory, though. He said, "This falls neatly under 'nothing is ever perfect.'"

My John is a realist.

Just a few days later, I found Eli looking at Bengal websites. He was looking at the silver spotteds this time. Zoë had been the dramatic orangey color, and he wanted a brand-new relationship on its own terms.

We had Miss Sadie by Christmas vacation. She's an F4, which means she is a little wilder than Zoë had been. She has that low-slung tiger belly. We used to have mice in the attic occasionally. Then we got Sadie. For a while, she brought us one every day. With the pride of the hunter, she took them to each of us. She put one on each of the dog's beds. She is totally bonded to our dogs. The dogs are her very best friends, her brother and sisters, really, come to that.

And so that was how the whole yelling thing happened.

She was howling. Really howling. It was loud. The dogs were out for a walk and Sadie had been left behind. She hates that.

Our friend David Silver was visiting. He had, perhaps, had enough. He had been warned about the howling. I mean, I'd explained about her feelings of dislocation lately. She was adjusting to some changes in her environment, and this little . . . umm . . . behavior. Well, we were trying to ignore it. We figured that if we gave it no energy, it would resolve itself. Or possibly we'd buy ear-plugs.

Anyway, David had had a wee bit of gin that afternoon. He must have thought he was alone. Eli was fishing, and John was walking the dogs, ergo the cat howling. To be fair, it was quite a high-pitched and protracted howling that would happen every single time the dogs went on a walk without Sadie. Every time.

I was supposed to be taking a nap. Only, I was awake. And my friend David is not so quiet, either.

Anyway, there was howling and more howling. It was a screeching, distressed *Meowaieeeeee* over and over again. I'd started to just tune it out. And then I heard an equally distressed David howl, "Shut up! You are a fucking cat!"

Well then.

This really put a damper on the whole visit. I raced down the stairs past my scared kitty, who was by then racing up the stairs. I calmly asked David, "Are you drunk, or do you just hate cats?"

There was a bit of a verbal scuffle. He did try to apologize. Sort of. I might not have accepted it with grace.

And so for a while we were on a sort of mutual time-out. John and I were holding our little grudges and our friend was sweetly calling and emailing. Truth is we had been on a bad run and so maybe there was some overreacting going on. We almost talked about it, but not quite. We spoke only of a little bump, maybe a rub. I suggested we let time do its thing, to which David responded that he was "better at ignoring a problem and doing nothing than practically anyone in the whole world."

I loved that, of course.

We still loved him, too. I figured we were going to have to make up pretty soon. And so, pretty soon we did. We did, because, you know, this is what you do in a real friendship of long duration. You scooch over and make room for one another's foibles. By the time you hit middle age, you learn that you don't get to only be friends with perfect people or you'd have no friends at all. No one would want us as friends either, come to think of it. And anyway, this was the guy who had negotiated our Peltier's sale in a time of great distress. I would remember that forever. I figured that bought him a lot of scooching over. And come to think of it, he'd forgiven me a time or two as well.

But I might not leave him alone with my cat again. Ever.

ooooo

With Sadie to help out at home, we hired our good friend, the brilliant Dr. Lynda Katz, to do the memory testing that Eli clearly needed. Lynda was president of Landmark College, which is the nation's premier college for kids who learn differently. She's a top neuropsychologist. The best.

She called me as soon as she had his scores.

"Ellen, it must have been the Lyme." She was compassionate, but clear. "His memory scores are very, very low. He doesn't know the stuff someone growing up in your family, with his frame of reference, ought to know."

It was a confirmation of something we had all begun to realize. Things were different now.

The neurologists we consulted explained that lesions in the white brain matter often repair. He had six. Puberty and adolescence and the increasing hormones might slow down the repairs. We could accommodate the condition for now. And school? Well, school had stopped being fun.

We were very lucky in one respect. That respect was Colleen Fiore. Colleen was Eli's learning specialist. She had been Hannah's homeroom advisor years before. We knew her and her family well. Colleen is one of those teachers who are born, not made. She is a virtuoso. She is kind and smart. She's the sort of creative problem solver who sees fifty solutions to every puzzle. If you have a learning difference, you want Colleen in your corner. Eli loved her. John and I adored her. She and Eli spent several hours together every week.

But it wasn't enough.

There was one history teacher, in particular, that seemed to lecture unendingly, making himself the center of the classroom. Learning didn't seem to be a big priority. Rather than inspiring students, he was one of life's correctors.

"Ha ha! No, that's not right. It happened on October 8, 1891!"

History suffered under his banal gaze.

"No."

"No."

"Wrong."

"Wrong day."

"Wrong. Wrong. Wrong."

Rote memorization was apparently the only worthwhile way to learn about all that had come before. Instead of building up, this class was all about tearing down and boring the students practically to death.

Now, imagine if you had a little memory problem. In addition to being bored, you might start to feel stupid.

It was a cocktail for disaster.

We tried, though. We had teacher conferences to talk about the accommodations Eli needed now. We knew this was going to be hard for everyone, but we wanted to make sure that we had a plan. We added assistive technology to Eli's toolbox. His fine motor skills, which had never been great, had suffered after the illness. His handwriting was completely illegible now. He carried a laptop to class, but speed was an issue. He had a smartpen that allowed him to tape lectures and return to any given point that he wanted to listen to again.

I asked the "unimaginative" history teacher for his lecture notes. The instructor was also, apparently, quite lazy.[12] He explained that he didn't produce class notes. It seems he said something different each time he taught the course.[13] But he said that Eli could get the notes from other kids in his class. Or from one of the other classes as well.

"If you never say the same thing twice, won't the notes from the other classes be different?" I more or less innocently asked. The other teachers in the conference may have snickered.

He then said, I swear in exactly these words, "If he can't remember anything anyway maybe he could skip history this year."

Oh boy.

I was off.

---

12. Banal and lazy so often go neatly together, in my experience.

13. Sure he did. Though apparently he had amazing recall for someone so quick to chastise students as "Wrong!"

The other teachers seemed to scoot back from the table. Maybe they expected me to turn it over? That might not have been a bad move, actually. Instead, I lowered my voice and began talking . . . quietly, slowly, and clearly. It might have been a frightening quiet.

"The point to history, sir, is not to remember the dates of battles. It is to learn and internalize broad cultural and civic patterns and motivations. It is about critical evaluation. The point to history is to learn *how* to think, not *what* to think."

I had been on the board of trustees for this school for five years. I had raised money for it, served hundreds of hours on the search committee for a new head of school, and on the strategic planning committee. John volunteered to help the soccer program before eventually becoming a coach and teaching here. Hannah had been a National Honor Society student who babysat for the teachers. We were a part of this community, a member of this family. How was it that we had managed to hire a headmaster who permitted this level of incompetence and ignorance on the teaching staff? I was so mad I could have spit.[14]

It wasn't a pretty meeting. I imagine it looked a lot different to that history teacher. It certainly had an impact on me. Education is important, and it seems to me that we're all in it together: teachers, parents, and students. There just isn't room for folks who are more interested in their own convenience than their students' education.

We got through that year, of course, as one does. Eli was brave. Colleen was our guardian angel. It turned out, of course, that Eli had been right. This was not the school for him. This was a school for a

---

14. Or peed. I began to imagine peeing on this man's chair. Our whole family could take turns. This fantasy made me enormously happy. There was a crime spree in the making.

narrow range of students. Those students risked being systematically dumbed down by the likes of this history teacher.

Okay, I was generalizing like mad. You learn a lot about teaching ability when you have a problem. Every teacher looks great when their students are successful kids who could learn in a dark closet with a flashlight. Less so when trouble rears its head.

Everyone in the student services office was terrific, though. They shared war stories about the teachers that they battled. Which, of course, begged the question. How could that happen? In a world where 25 percent of Americans have learning differences, how could a progressive independent school not have a workforce trained to teach students with differences? People who learn differently are some of the brightest creative minds we have. As a nation, we want them at the table.

Make no mistake, there were many wonderful teachers. Sean and his wife, Alicia, were treasures. Nate and Erin brought love and life to history and science in the middle school. Anharad and Tracey made art and theater sing for kids. Jim and Michelle brought English and math to life. But they should have been the rule, not the exception.

Sure, we had complained on occasion before. In another year, it had been a condescending math teacher.[15] But now I knew the truth and there was no going back. Long Trail wasn't for everybody. Not even for families who had been there for eight years. It was no longer our school.

Eli had his sophomore year at BBA.

ooooo

---

15. Although we sort of lost the moral high ground when Eli . . . well, you know.

SCRAPS

My friend Karen has the biggest table I know.

Her already-large family just keeps getting bigger. There are kids and grandkids. Boyfriends and girlfriends. Nieces and nephews. In-laws and outlaws. Their family is huge.

Karen is handy, and every time someone gets married or adopts a baby she just adds a little more to the table. Once when I was visiting, I saw half a dozen people sitting around working on their laptops. There was a child making art, and another one eating a bowl of cereal. It was a place where they could all sort of parallel play, getting their individual work done but being together, safe in one another's presence. Our kitchen is like that too. We naturally gravitate to the kitchen table. Eli does homework while John and I work on our laptops.

We play cards and backgammon there. When the big kids are home, we squeeze up to the table and everybody does their thing. Someone reads the paper while someone else reads a book. There is almost always someone fiddling with music on an iPod and pretty soon one of us gets up and makes some food. Julia Reed wrote a book a while ago called *Ham Biscuits, Hostess Gowns, and Other Southern Specialties*. In it, she shared several recipes for pimento cheese. We often have a big bowlful of it sitting on the table.

We also love olives, and I might make a kielbasa sliced thin and painted with tallegio on a plate piled high with olives or cornichons. The snacking is part of what keeps people in the room. That, and the company. Quality time is not something you arrange. The big conversations do not happen on the day you planned the outing. They happen over a mouthful of cheese or a game of backgammon. Proximity is a big part of what keeps this family . . . well . . . "together."

After Eli got sick, we all came around the table for a while. We just wanted to be together and maybe see him fatten up a little. Normally, it is the chickens that get all of our scraps. They sit outside the kitchen window and we toss them leftover potatoes and bread.[1] The dogs lobby pretty hard, too. But for a while that year it was Eli.

We plied him with thick malted milkshakes and eggy brioche. Every cold day was an excuse for spicy hot cocoa. Even the big kids were in on it. Benjamin brought him bagels and cream cheese at school. Hannah came home and made chocolate chip cookie dough. No cookies, mind you. Just a giant-sized bowl of dough. It was gone in a flash.

The table was full of creamy things like mashed potatoes with real cream and Parmesan that year. I made cupcakes every Sunday night for twelve months. Before long, he was just "normal skinny" again. And in the meantime, those ginger cupcakes with the maple glaze became a staple.[2]

ooooo

---

1. Chickens, it turns out, really love their carbs.

2. None of this was particularly good for my already ample backside. I mean, you have to taste the food you serve, right? I licked a lot of spatulas that year. And maybe . . . well, there was really no maybe about it, it showed.

CHAPTER SIX

Steve

"I WANNA COME AND SEE THE POND, TOO. CAN I COME NEXT summer if you guys get a place again?"

Steve had come for another quick visit to fish with Benjamin, and to see Eli after the difficulties of the summer. Everyone just wanted to touch Eli. To make sure he was still with us, and getting better. We were all worried.

As I have often said, Steve and I had been married for about fifteen minutes a quarter century earlier, but nothing about our relationship then could have predicted our family now. Luckily, we had both improved with age. Taking a vacation together didn't seem weird. It seemed sort of normal, actually.[1]

Everyone knows that I remarried well. My marriage to John is one of the best things about me. And Steve, John, and I were a long-seasoned parenting team. Steve came to every one of Benjamin's soccer games. John coached and Steve cheered as loudly for the coach as he did for his son. He jumped and hollered at basketball games. And he called to say goodnight every single day for thirteen years. Eventually, teenage Benjamin felt too old for the nightly calls and told Steve that he could stop. When we all lived in Edwardsville, Steve had supper at our house two or three times every week. He was our babysitter on date night. Hannah and Eli always called him Uncle Steve. Truth be told, we *were* all a little bit like an Alan Alda movie.

---

1. Which I do realize is a little weird. I do.

Steve knew me when I was just barely out of Granite City. I hadn't learned how to own a business, and I couldn't have imagined the life I would end up with. Steve proudly told our story to anyone who would listen. In a way, he was more like a brother to me than a former husband.

○○○○○

So Steve was visiting us in Vermont after Eli's illness and we were all on blankets looking up at the stars, recounting the summer we'd just had on the island. Eli had gotten sick, but Benjamin had found new passions, fly fishing and now hunting. Like practically everything, it was a mixed bag.

Steve was enthusiastic. As always.

"Has Benjamin done any ocean fishing yet? I have a bunch of books about stripers and bonita. We could go to Orvis and get some ocean flies. I might have a fly rod that would be perfect for those fast little false albacores. Can you rent a fishing boat? I really want to come. When do you think you will go?" It was all one long sentence.

We agreed that, of course, he would come.

John and Steve started discussing where to fly and how best to get to the boat. Steve loved gear and logistics better than just about anything. He had more coats and vests and hats than anybody you will ever meet. The man was an Orvis catalog. Gardening, fishing, or cutting the lawn . . . everything required planning and costume changes. Steve always had just the right hat.

Steve was also a great naturalist. He introduced our kids to geodes, and to all the flora and fauna in the woods. When we moved to Vermont, we figured it was just a matter of time before he would, too. He was starting to talk about retiring up here, now that it looked like we were here to stay. I guess he was waiting to see whether the Horrible Quaint Country Store episode would sour us on Dorset. It hadn't, so talk of moving seemed reasonable.

On his last trip here, he had gone fly-fishing with Bejamin in the Mettowee River behind Benjamin's house. Since Steve had come up for Benjamin's college graduation the year before, they had been getting into a fishing groove together. Benjamin shares some of our more . . . excitable . . . personality traits. So he and Steve had never been exactly at ease with one another. Benjamin was the really smart, wildly ADHD kid whom you could not take your eyes off of for even a minute. Steve was the guy who couldn't relax. It was an imperfect combination. The vigilance required during the early years was often more than Steve could summon, and so they spent time together best when the rest of us were there as a buffer. It was really a family affair. Now as Benjamin had begun to come into himself as an adult, they were feeling easier around each other. It had taken years, but it was sweet to see.

As they fished, Benjamin had brought up his newest hobby: bird hunting. When Steve got home to St. Louis from this visit, the bird-hunting emails started in hard and heavy. Benjamin's bird hunting was not the sit-in-a-blind Vermont-style turkey hunting or learn-to-use-a-call duck hunting. This was, rather, the kind of bird hunting that was a race through the woods with well-trained dogs. The race was followed by getting on an airplane, so that you could then traipse around the country looking for more quail and grouse. That sort of hunting. It costs a fortune to support and apparently it was all the rage in the banking set. But Benjamin, like Steve, is enthusiastic about his pursuits.

Benjamin had started his own filmmaking business[2] and was having great success at it. As far as I could see, he was mostly using

---

2. His company, Almost Blue Productions, makes affecting microdocumentaries for organizations, which use them to tell their stories in pictures. It is a lovely mixture of sales and art.

the business to support all these new expensive habits he was acquiring. He would call to announce a new client he'd nabbed. Before I could even get the congratulations out, he'd be talking about the fishing or hunting gear it would pay for.

Despite moving to a liberal state with equally liberal gun laws and a whole population who grew up shooting, I had not imagined that I would ever raise a hunter.

When our kids were little, we had very definite ideas about what their raising was going to look like. There would be no gender biases in our toy purchases, for one thing. We were not going to fall into the truck-and-gun or pink-and-purple trap. Our house would be free of the stereotyping messages that our culture bombards little boys and girls with on TV and on the playground. Our house would be a gender-neutral zone, where preferences and natural identity were respected and exploration of biases examined. Multiculturalism would be taught and thoughtful discourse would be encouraged. This was the way we made our way in the world and it was the way we would raise our children, by golly.

We had spent lots of time thinking about these issues and planning our parenting styles. Our ideas had been long considered, and we were going to wind up with balanced kids who treated everyone they met with kindness, dignity, and respect. They would not be bound by society's notions of male and female. Their lives would be fuller and richer as a result. I'm sure we saw them bringing peace to the Middle East and curing cancer while they were at it.

In the whole nature-versus-nurture debate, we fell squarely on the nurture side. We figured if parents would just provide loving experiences and offer up ideas at the supper table, kids would gravitate toward tolerance. What debate? We had this whole thing figured out.

Only then, we actually met the kids. We had forgotten that they might come to the party with their own ideas.

I began to get an inkling of the problem when Benjamin was about three. We'd gotten him a baby doll for Christmas. I was pregnant with Hannah, and the doll, Baby Sarah, was to be his baby. She was a beautiful African American baby with soft milk-chocolatey skin. He chose her himself from a wide shelf of offerings. I was smug and proud as we walked to the checkout counter. There were happy thought-bubbles bouncing all around:

This really works!

He picked a *black* baby.

He doesn't even see color differences.

I was so proud I could hardly stand it.

Now, we had very limited television watching. Benjamin was a Big Bird fan, so *Sesame Street* was on the list. *The World of David the Gnome* had just come out, and I loved those sweet little cartoons with the fox who raced through the forest. So that made the list, too. But there was no violent television in our house. John and I didn't watch much TV anyway, so this was easy.

We had no war toys, either. Benjamin played with other kids at the playground, but that was all about the slide and feeding ducks in the pond. He had the sweetest little childhood experiences I could have dreamt up.

When we got home with Baby Sarah that day, I started fixing supper. Steve had come over early and went outside to watch Benjamin play. Imagine my surprise when I went out to the yard with a little pre-supper snack. Benjamin had given Baby Sarah a drink from the hose. That was thoughtful. But he noticed that her belly filled with water when she "drank." He quickly added some little rocks to the belly. When I came out with apples and peanut butter, he was squeezing her belly and making AK-47 sounds. He was shooting . . . make that SHOOTING! the rocks out of her mouth by squeezing her middle. Sounds were coming from the back of his throat that were remarkably like a fast-shooting gun.

"*Aa aa aa aa aa! Aa aa aa aa aa!*" Three years old and impro-vising a machine gun from a baby doll and a water hose. Well, at least I raised a really smart, creative kid. And then I looked at Steve. Because surely that was the root of the problem, right?

"Steve, have you been playing gun games with Benjamin?!"

"No, I swear. Ellen, I swear. Really. I SWEAR!" He was des-perate that I believe him.

I didn't, of course. Where else could this shit be coming from?

"Benjamin, honey. Let's give Baby Sarah some apples."

"*Aa aa aa aa aa! Aa aa aa aa aa!*" Infantry Toddler.

Well, okay. So it was an aberration. A blip. And probably Steve's fault, anyway.

Then, of course, we met Hannah.

I bought her blue dresses, and a pile of trucks along with the dolls and chemistry sets.

By the time she was three, she was in all pink, all the time. By four, we gave up completely.

She had a Barbie car that she could drive, and when she spent the night with her friend Nora, the Barbie suitcase took up more room than her own clothes. When she had first started lobbying for Barbies, I carefully explained how Barbie's body didn't look like a real girl's body. Today, at twenty-three, Hannah is six feet tall and has a slim elegance. She has always been built like a racehorse. Ben-jamin listened at the table as I introduced good feminist theory to toddler Hannah.

"Mom," he breathed in exasperation. "Look at Hannah. I mean it. Really look. She does sort of look like a Barbie. Except her feet aren't pointed, I guess."

I looked.

"But, honey, women come in all shapes and sizes, and I don't

want Hannah growing up thinking we all need to look like Barbie."
I figured he could use a dose of feminism while I was serving it up.

Benjamin understood then where I was going with this. He was
her big brother, and he had just wanted to help. But he was on a roll.

He looked his sister in the eye and said, "Hannah, Mom's
right. You can probably have a Barbie, but you have to remember
that real people don't have pointy feet. They just do that so you can
get the shoes on."

He turned to me. "How about that, Mom. Can she have one
now?"

Sure. What the hell. I guess I couldn't blame it all on Steve.

These kids were supposed to have their own goddamned preferences, after all.

So we bought her a Barbie. I figured if I made too much of a
deal out of this she would get all obsessive about them. Buying her
one would curb her appetite. So we got one.

Pretty soon we had dozens. I was spending hours on the floor
putting on Barbie dresses and making high ponytails out of impossibly little hair. Truth is, some of my happiest memories are from those
long, lazy Barbie days.

And before long her room was pink pink pink as far as the eye
could see.

By the time Eli came along, we had the full catastrophe. During
all this parenting, we had managed to hold only one line in the
battle. "The battle." See, even I'm doing it. Anyway, during this
particular battle, we permitted colorful water guns *only*. Nothing
realistic-looking.

I ought to get to have some preferences of my own, damn it. I
was standing my ground.

Then we moved to Vermont when Eli was seven. Vermont,
where even our liberal PhD friends bought Winchesters from cab-

drivers and ran blood trails in the dark. There was something in the air. So we were in Vermont, where every kid for miles had "airsoft" guns. Airsoft guns are plastic guns that look so real, they would get you arrested in an airport.

These things shoot bullets that are bigger and softer than BBs, but not quite as soft as Nerf balls. One afternoon, Timmy's dad brought Eli home because they were going to have an "airsoft war" and Eli had explained to them, with great sadness, that he wasn't allowed to play with guns. And possibly that his parents are the worst. That he lives in an authoritarian state. And that he should probably go home in case there were spies. So Mike, without any judgment, sweetly and responsibly brought Eli home.

I started off feeling proud of our big seven-year-old boy for telling Mike about the family rules. Only, as he told me about the boys building the dirt hills for the war, he plaintively asked could he maybe just possibly go back for that part, with such longing in his eyes. I could stand my own principles no longer. We went to the sporting goods store and came home with three of the little devils.

For a while I made him paint the airsoft guns orange so they wouldn't look like real guns. This seemed like a fun activity that would help keep him safe. And perhaps more importantly, made me feel like we were making it clear that this was just a game. This was not shooting. It was more a kind of tag. Yes . . . well, I needed to tell myself something.

But the orange paint got all over everything. It also made Eli stand out in a way that meant he got shot more than anyone else. This didn't seem fair. And I might be a little competitive too. So before long, we had a passel of the blackest, realest-looking guns in the village. I mean, I didn't want my kid to lose the battle, for God's sakes. That would be wrong. And against my principles.

Come autumn, I was hosting airsoft wars of our own, complete with BBQ pork sandwiches for the ceasefires. We also added a shooting, screaming banshee of a mother, who decided when the time-out was over. And who got the first shots off herself, before they had finished chewing their sandwiches.

Parenting is a full-contact sport.

Surprisingly now, lo these many years later, I still had the same knee-jerk reactions I'd always had about guns, when our friend Bob first invited Benjamin to go grouse hunting.

"Bob, you have no idea how ADHD Benjamin is. Really, he has no attention span. No training with guns. Do you really want to take him hunting?"

Turns out, he did. And besides, the kid was in his twenties by then. He was a man. This was really none of my business. So mostly I just worried.

Steve had hunted when he was younger, but he had always been more of a fly-fishing angler than a hunter. Plus, he had always been hesitant to introduce Benjamin to hunting given my . . . well, my tiny, little, hardly worth mentioning, really, feelings on the subject. And Benjamin had always been so ADD that we were all sure that he would shoot himself. Or somebody else. I wasn't interested in my boy bearing any resemblance to Dick Cheney.

Steve had all the "stuff" though. Gobs of guns. Hundreds of books about guns. And tons of books about bird hunting. The thing is that Steve had always relished studying a subject almost more than actually engaging in it. He was an avid armchair traveler and hunter and fisherman. He had a houseful of the accoutrements of his hobbies. Hobbies that he really only spent a few days a year doing. But he spent hundreds of hours in deep contemplation of his next trip, and in polishing up all of the specialty equipment which he just had to have to do the thing properly.

Steve was delighted when Benjamin said he was going quail

hunting with our friend Bob Lewis.[3]

John and I mostly just fretted.

Bob's plan was that Benjamin would come along with him and just watch for the first day. He was being cautious. It was a reasonable, thoughtful plan. Well, that lasted until they drove by the country store that sold the licenses, apparently.

Everyone in the truck decided that Benjamin better be licensed up, just in case he wanted to shoot at targets. Maybe he'd just hold one of the guns. And since you never know when you might meet a ranger in the woods, it was better to be safe than sorry. Bob decided to bring along a second gun just for that eventuality.

Everyone piled back into the truck and headed out to quail country. When they reached their spot, the guide showed Benjamin how to hold the gun and the basics of how to shoot. Here's the safety. Here's how to load it. Here's how to aim. Squeeze the trigger, don't pull it. That sort of thing.

Big surprise. The kid was a natural. I sort of pictured him trying to load the gun with a water hose and a bunch of little rocks. But apparently he had a feel for the whole thing. I guess those hundreds of hours of video gaming over the years connected to some natural talent. And then they put a gun in his hands. Well, of course they let him hunt with the rest of the group.

Bob is a responsible, thoughtful man who spent a long time telling Benjamin that whether he got a shot at a bird that day would be something that he might or might not remember. But if he shot one of those beautiful hunting dogs, or, God forbid, one of the men in the party . . . well, that he would never forget. Bob doled out lessons and cautions and pretty soon they were all on their way.

Of course, you probably can guess what happened next. The dogs pointed a grouse. Everyone raised guns. And Benjamin got the

---

3. Dan's dad: a man with elegant table manners.

first bird of the day. Of course he did. Bob was thrilled. The guides gushed.

"Listen, man, you have no idea what you just did." They wanted him to appreciate the gravity of his success.

"Oh, man! I mean it. This is really amazing. This never happens."

Bob said, "Benjamin, this is just wonderful. Son, you have a real story to tell your grandkids. *Nobody* gets a grouse on their first try."

The hunters came home that night with a sackful of birds. Benjamin had one grouse and two woodcocks by the end of the day. He also had an abiding passion for bird hunting.

Before long, I was looking up grouse recipes. I was doing my part. Steve and the young hunter were on the phone all the time talking about gunstocks and bird dogs.

In short order, it became clear that this was a sport that needed a dog. Sure, you could hire guides and their dogs, but that was expensive. It also meant that this would be only an occasional "gentlemen's hobby." After a couple more trips, it was clear that bird hunting would be much more than an occasional adventure. It was all Benjamin thought about.

"Mom, bird hunting is made for the ADD brain," he explained. "You are constantly scanning and you have to have rapid reflexes. Plus, you get to be in the woods walking in beautiful spots. You look for the food you know the grouse eat and the cover they like. This sport is made for me." Well, I couldn't argue that.

He started writing beautiful essays about the woods and the morning mist. The experience took over his thinking like first loves do.

And so it was quickly decided. Benjamin needed a dog. First of all, he had moved out after graduating from college and he missed living with our pack of animals. But possibly of greater importance, he wanted to have a hunting buddy in the woods. After Steve left

Vermont and was back home in Edwardsville, he began the research in earnest. Not a day went by that my inbox wasn't filled with dogs. Steve and Benjamin had narrowed the search to about three different, and to my ears, fairly exotic, breeds. Steve loved researching gear and this was gear on a whole new level. Gear that barked.

Benjamin, who is a generous and loving young man, had in mind what he really wanted, but he could see that his dad was getting excited. So he extended and expanded the search to include his new research partner. In the meantime, our post office box was filling fast with flyers and highlighted magazine articles. Pictures of guns and dogs. And then, actual guns.

Alarmingly, Steve had an old collection of guns. He was refinishing stocks and sending them along at a shocking rate. Hannah was set to graduate from college in the spring, and Steve was planning on coming in for that occasion. He was bringing a gun case and a new ocean rod for Benjamin to consider. I figured something would go wrong and the FBI would wind up at the party, but Steve would probably have brought the drinks along with him, so surely that would end well.

In the meantime, the two of them were hot on the scent of the dog. They finally decided that Benjamin was getting an Italian Spinone. They are fairly rare in this country, and he wanted a female brown-and-white roan, which is even harder to come by. But there was a puppy in North Carolina. She was four months old and the breeder had been hoping to keep her. She was the pick of the litter. Only, unfortunately, financial calamity had come. The breeder was selling her house and moving. The puppy had to go. This was all very sad for the breeder, but felt like our lucky day.

Benjamin had been in touch with practically every Spinone breeder in the United States, and they all knew what he wanted. Several called to tell him that this girl was coming available. John had a long spring break coming up, so he and Benjamin decided to make the flight together to pick her up. Steve was saving his vacation for Hannah's graduation and a trip to the island with us in July. Since it would likely be messy, and potentially stressful, traveling with a puppy, John was the designated calm traveler for the pickup trip.

Not me.

Certainly not Steve.

Benjamin had to go, since she would be his dog. And somehow we knew that John would make it all work. He always does.

Bags were packed and the boys were almost headed out the door. In his carry-on, Benjamin had the collar and leash in case he got separated from his main bag. But then he decided he should also have some doggie treats with him, so he ran out to the pet store in Manchester. John's bags were already in the car. In fifteen minutes they would be on their way and soon we would have a new member of the family. It felt like we were about to have our first grandchild. There had been so much preparation and planning, and just that week he'd decided on her name.

Olive.

Benjamin wanted a name that reminded him of Italy, but all of the Italian names were too multisyllabic for a hunting girl in the woods. So he'd settled on Olive and we were all ready. I ran upstairs to look for John's cell phone just as the phone in the kitchen rang. John grabbed it, figuring on telling Benjamin to hurry up or they'd be late for the plane.

It wasn't Benjamin.

It was Aunt Mindy, Steve's sister.

John handed me the phone.

My oldest son's father, Stephen Russell Stimson III, died suddenly on March 11, 2011, of a rare heart arrhythmia. He died wearing his favorite hat while doing a little spring cleanup in the yard.

ooooo

CHAPTER SEVEN

Pants Matter

THE NEXT FEW DAYS PASSED IN A SAD BLUR. OLIVE'S FIRST TRIP to Vermont was postponed. First, we had a memorial service to plan. John and I knew in an instant that we were facing a huge parenting challenge. And this time, there would just be the two of us to do it. Our son, all of our children, really, had lost one of the main people in their lives.

Grief.

This is one of the things parents are supposed to be able to teach their kids how to do. But surely not now. This was something, if we had thought about at all, we figured would be a part of the future. We barely knew how to deal with grief ourselves.

My dad died when I was five years old, so I don't really remember him. At five, there probably was not much in the way of regular grieving, either. John lost his dad when he was fourteen. He probably knew more than I did about grieving. But he had been young for his age, growing up. Fourteen is still so very young, anyway. I'd lost both of my grandmothers when I was a teenager and didn't remember learning much about grief either time. They were both old ladies who'd had good long lives. I'd cried some, but my life had not been truly disrupted in any major way.

Then there was my mom. I'd lost my mom in January of 2008. Steve was there when John and the kids and I landed in St. Louis. He was there with Mindy and our friends, too. Friends always turn up in sad times, but this time there was an especially tight posse wrapping their arms around all of us. They worried it might be especially hard.

My mom and I had not enjoyed a close, loving relationship for a long time. There had been an old family trouble that divided us. When she died I was sad. But mostly I was sad not to have had the mother-daughter relationship that I'd wished I'd had. So the only real death I had ever experienced had been a mixed bag of sadness and regret. The mourning and the grief had been long in the making. My mother's death did not hasten it in any significant way.

Losing Steve was, in a way, the first normal human loss I'd ever had. When I took the phone from John, I was already crying. So was he. We both knew Benjamin would be running in the door ready to get on the flight any time now. How do you tell your young adult child one of his parents has died? There was no time for a crash course on grieving. We did not have a map, but we were going on the trip.

ooooo

Benjamin crashed through the door and ripped off his pants. He called out, "The dryer didn't dry these pants completely."

He ran through the house in his boxers. At least he wasn't naked.

"I know, I know," he said when he saw our faces. He figured we were set to gripe about how late they were going to be for the plane to North Carolina.

"We'll make it up on the road. We have two whole hours. I have to go to the bathroom." He hustled through the house. "Just give my pants five minutes. They weren't dry and I do not want to sit on a plane with cold wet legs."

John and I blinked.

We'd hung up with Mindy when we heard his car in the driveway. We started to follow him into the living room.

The phone rang.

I was wobbly.

John answered, and it was Hannah.

"Why aren't you guys on the road? When are you leaving?" she asked.

Hannah was headed home for the beginning of spring break. Dan had picked her up so he could see her before she and a bunch of her girlfriends headed off on a trip. John handed me the phone, shaking his head.

Deep breaths.

"Hi, sweetie," I sighed.

She started in on one long run-on sentence. She was filling me in on where they were on the road—that they would be stopping at the mall to look for a new swimsuit for her trip—and why hadn't Dad and Benjamin left yet? I interrupted.

"Honey, something terrible has happened. We need you to come home first before you go anywhere else."

Silence.

"Ohmygod. What's wrong? Did Grandma Dorothy die?"

She loved her Grandma Dorothy.

"No, honey. But it's bad. Are you driving?"

"No, Dan is. What, Mommy?" Her voice was already quivering. "Is it Eli again?"

"Sweetie . . . Steve just died."

"Ohmygod." Pause.

"Ohmygod. Does Baba know?"

Baba had been the nickname she'd given her brother when she was little and couldn't pronounce "Benjamin" yet. She was in her twenties, but now I was Mommy and he was Baba. This was going to be hard.

"What happened?" she asked.

"It looks like a heart attack, honey. Baba just got here now. I have to tell him. Come home, honey. We'll all be together. Tell Dan to drive slow."

She whispered goodbye and said she'd be here soon.

As soon as we put the phone down, it rang again. John picked it up again. This time it was Eli. It was like they'd all gotten the same signal at the exact same moment.

"Hey, Dad . . ."

Wordlessly John handed over the phone and headed toward the library, where Benjamin would soon be coming out.

I explained for the second time what was happening and Eli said he was on his way.

Meanwhile, Benjamin came into the room and looked at our faces.

"What?" he huffed.

"Honey, we need to talk." The soft, motherly tone seemed to cue him that something was going on.

"What?" he asked again.

"Sweetie, we have had some really bad news."

"*What?* Just tell me." He thought about it for a second. "What? Where's Eli?"

"Eli's fine." We all still had a little posttraumatic shock from the illness over the summer.

"Honey, this is really hard. Your dad died."

My voice broke. I couldn't keep it together. We walked toward him to wrap our arms around him.

"NO! Steve? No."

He backed away. Almost angry.

"No, he didn't. Why are you saying this?"

"Oh, Baba . . ." John put an arm around him.

"Sweetie, he did. Aunt Mindy just called."

"Where are my pants?"

Well, yeah. He wasn't wearing pants, and this was a lot to take in.

Benjamin headed to the dryer to get his damp pants. He came back in without them and collapsed into our arms. We all sort of staggered over to the couch, hugging and crying.

He was too young to have to face this. Aren't we all, really? His relationship with Steve had just begun to click. They had found this wonderful new language together.

Shitshitshit.

Now what?

Well now, we cry.

Hannah came in after a while, and she joined us on the couch. Eli came right after.

We cried until we ran out.

Then Benjamin remembered the puppy.

"We've got to call the breeder. Poor little Olive. She was supposed to come home today." His concern was pretty clearly channeling itself somewhere that it might do some good.

Eli responded, "She's a puppy. The extra week might not mean much to her."

For some reason, the idea of a puppy who didn't understand time struck us all as funny. Like she knew she was coming and was eagerly waiting for that, but, you know, the extra week wouldn't really matter all that much. It wasn't going to throw off her complicated social calendar or anything. We all started laughing then.

And right in the middle of a breath Hannah said, "Benjamin, I think you are going to need some pants."

He was wearing a nice purple Robert Graham shirt over a brick-colored tee and boxers with Tigger on them.

Tigger. From Winnie the Pooh.

Really.

We all looked at him. And, actually, that was pretty funny, too. So we looked for his pants. And couldn't find them. They weren't in the dryer. Where in the hell were his pants? Eli looked in the bathroom. Hannah looked in the kitchen.

Benjamin was looking under the couch when he said, "I cannot have a dead dad and no pants."

That cracked us all up. Even Dan joined in the laughter. He was still very new around our family and probably didn't know what to do with a brand-new girlfriend whose pantsless brother's dad had died. Well, would anyone, now that I think about it?

All of a sudden though, Benjamin was looking mad.

We all stopped laughing.

We didn't know what we were supposed to do, but as a family we mirrored Benjamin's emotions and we looked for those pants. Where *were* those damned pants?!

We were all over the map. A mess.

Finally, someone looked in the dining room. They were on the table. The scorched and sanded dining room table. When had he gone into the dining room?

Benjamin dressed. Which seemed to be the cue that we could all start crying again.

With our pants on.

ooooo

Benjamin and I got to Steve's house on a Friday. Mindy drove us over and we sat in the driveway together. Mindy is the aunt every child should have. She had been at every basketball game, every play, and every birthday the whole time we lived in St. Louis for all three kids for all of their lives. And she flew to Vermont for graduations and all the important celebrations now. She is wonderful. Now she sat with us in Steve's driveway.

We sat there a long time. Her quiet presence was just right. John, Eli, and Hannah were flying in behind us. John was making the arrangements for the dogs and the chickens, while Benjamin and

I came ahead to arrange the memorial service. And John was writing the eulogy.

The night before as we sat in the library together at home, Benjamin wondered if he would be expected to give the eulogy at the service. But it was all so raw. So fresh. Benjamin couldn't imagine doing that. So he turned to the only other person he could envision doing it. He told John that he should give the eulogy from our family. John had simply wrapped his arms around our boy, nodded, picked up his computer, and gone to work.

When we pulled up to the house, I stuck my head into Steve's car first. I almost couldn't catch my breath. I mean, there he was. Well, there he was in so many ways. There was a leather journal with drawings and lists next to a pair of binoculars and a pile of maps with turned-down corners and markings all over them. He had always seemed to have a dozen apothecary-type potions with him, smelling of Bay Rum and spice. That car smelled just like him. I just kept asking myself, How could this be happening? Our boy was twenty-six. Steve's life had just gotten to the good part. I could barely keep standing up.

But of course, I did. My boy needed me.

I think that no matter how old, how adult, my kids get, they will still be my boys and my girl. It's part of this parenting thing. At twenty-six, he seemed so young in my eyes. I was the grownup here.

As we went into the house, we were looking right at Steve's dining room table. There was a gunstock he'd been refinishing for Benjamin. There was a box with a necklace of his grandmother's he'd been planning to have restrung for Hannah's graduation. Binoculars littered every surface. Magazine articles about hunting dogs were strewn around. There was a book about learning Chinese in a week.[1]

---

1. Funny, I always thought it would take longer.

There were recipes. Piles of books. The smell of Bay Rum and old leather. Fishing rods and coats. The jumble and accumulation of one man's life.

Upstairs, we saw the pictures. All of our kids and our lives were on every shelf. Benjamin had not played a college basketball game that his dad hadn't tracked. The newspaper clippings were all neatly organized and bound into albums. There were our family pictures . . . everywhere. Here in this private space it was completely clear.

We were Steve's family. His adored son, former wife, her husband, and their kids. This was a man who had loved all of us, and we'd all loved him back.

Mindy helped us write the obituary, and the next day, when John gave his eulogy, there wasn't a dry eye in the room.

This is a sad time for our family. Steve has always been a part of the group, and he's been there for most of our special milestones—births, deaths, graduations, birthday parties, holidays, and even a vacation or two. We all journeyed through difficult times together many years ago, mixed in with the mundane, pleasant, loving experiences; and we all—Ellen and I, Benjamin, Hannah, and Eli, and our friends, old and new—came through to this comfortable place with Steve where everyone was able to easily enjoy one another's company, share in life's joys and sorrows, and help one another in time of need.

My mother, who is here today, lives nearby. Ellen and the kids and I live far away. Anytime my mom needed something or had a problem that required attending, it was Steve Stimson who would help her. On a regular basis over the last several years, Ellen or I could call Steve. He would drop whatever he was doing—which usually meant piddling around with some rare vine or fungi that he'd stumbled across (but sometimes he would actually be busy and the errand we requested would require that he change his plans)—Steve never failed. He took great pride, I think, in being more professional than FedEx or UPS. But most of all, Steve was a gentleman and a kind soul. He understood, and cared on a profound level, that someone needed help and he was in the position to help. Practically every Mother's Day and every birthday, when Ellen and I would leave it till the last minute—like so many of us do—Steve would step in happily to be the last leg on the delivery chain. Then he would call us from his cell phone while backing out of her driveway and say, "Okay, mission accomplished." I'm not sure what we're going to do now. Without Steve, if I hope to continue the charade of being a half-decent son, then I'm going to have to step it up somehow.

The most lasting connection Steve and I have is that we shared a son. Or, rather, Steve shared his son with me. That had to be extremely difficult and painful for him. I know that learning how to cope with one another in often less-than-ideal circumstances (whatever that means) made all of us better, stronger people. Benjamin was just two and a half when I came on the scene—a scene of tribulation for which I was unaccustomed. I was twenty-four. Just about everyone I knew wondered what I was thinking about. But, as demanding and awkward as those early years were and as remarkable and often comical as we all must have appeared, Steve and the rest of us worked diligently to keep our family moving forward, happy, healthy, and with good memories.

Steve was part of my family, and he welcomed me as

*part of his. I will always admire the inner strength he showed
as we all muddled our way through no man's land—an
image I'm sure Steve would appreciate.*

*I would say that all, or nearly all, of us here today had
the opportunity to see Steve's charm. We all know that he
was intelligent and an intellectual—a great lover of both
the arts and the sciences. But Steve was also charming and
a fine conversationalist. He could carry on a deep, mean-
ingful conversation with the brightest minds in the room or
chat respectfully and engagingly with someone in a corner
for whom social interaction was a chore. Even if he didn't
like you all that much he could still be charming. Now if he
loathed you . . . maybe you might not see the charming side
as readily.*

*We miss him. My whole family misses him already. We
missed him from the moment we heard he was gone. He had
become more than just a co-parent and former husband; he
was our friend; a welcome guest in our home—Steve loved
Vermont; and an important part of our lives. All of us
looked forward to spending more time with Steve. We were
all happy that he had come to a point in the last several years
where he was getting a great deal of enjoyment from life's
simple pleasures, and that he and Benjamin were connect-
ing in deep and loving ways—hunting, fishing, music, and
all manner of outdoor pursuits, as they did when Benjamin
was a little boy.*

*We should remember Steve dressed in all his special
gear, prepared for unimaginable disasters and emergen-
cies in the field: his vests lined with countless pockets and
zippers and flaps with three kinds of mosquito repellant;
his boots with the Gore-Tex lining (I had never heard of*

Gore-Tex before Steve); his knives; his herbs hanging like stalactites from the rafters of his kitchen; his multiple short-wave radios; his safari hats, fishing hats, and touring caps; driving around in his gold-colored Isuzu Trooper that had more portable dashboard controls than most jumbo jets. He also knew quite a bit about violent-crime statistics—even though he lived in Edwardsville most of his life.

In the old days Steve would get kind of excited about small things and wear us all out from time to time, but he never was anything but generous, honest, and loyal, and he tried very hard to be fair. These last ten years were a kind of renaissance for all of us. I am happy for Steve that he had a chance to see Benjamin become an independent young man and to spend time with him doing the things they both love; that he had become a close friend to Ellen; and that he remained a big part of my daughter Hannah's life, calling her on the phone often as she walked to class and lending an extra ear when she needed someone else to talk to.

Fifty-eight, as we know, is far, far too young. We can all take comfort that, when it was time for Steve to leave us, he was living a good life; involved in activities that gave him pleasure; and content in the knowledge that he had a close-knit group of friends and family who loved him and wished him well.

ooooo

STEVE'S TABLE

Steve's furniture was big and burly just like he was.

He liked the Arts and Crafts style of the end of the nineteenth and beginning of the twentieth centuries. His dining room table fit well into one of his previous houses and was crammed tightly into his last home. But it was a fixture that loomed as large as he did.

When we got to his house the weekend of the memorial service, that table was the first place we went. It was piled high with the activities and hobbies of an avid naturalist, sportsman, and collector. A devoted father and student of the arts and sciences. He was a damned committed hobbyist, or maybe a lay scientist. He loved to share his passions for botany, astronomy, optics, and history with all of us. He was also a passionate food and wine connoisseur.

That week, he was making stuff for Benjamin, considering learning Chinese, reading about spring flora, planning Hannah's graduation gift, studying trout waters, researching hunting dogs, and tying flies. All on that groaning table.

We sat and read and studied there. And then we went to the kitchen. There was a pile of dried mint on the counter, so I made a pot of tea with local honey. We sat drinking out of giant Henry the Eighth–style mugs, where else?

At the table.

CHAPTER EIGHT

Fur Comfort

WHEN THE KIDS WERE LITTLE AND THE WEATHER WOULD CHANGE over to winter, we would cuddle in our big bed and I would tell them that the north wind had come. We would snuggle under a pile of soft downy quilts, and the wind was our excuse for hot cocoa and ghost stories. In Kansas, they call them twisters. In the south of France, they call it the mistral. In New England, we call them Nor'easters.

Big wind. By whatever name.

Gale-force winds that run up one side of a mountain and come screaming down the other side, picking up speed as they go.

Our chickens tuck their heads under their wings and crowd together as close as they can get, puffing their feathers up and out as the howling starts. It is otherworldly, the sound of these big winds. And you can see it, too. The trees in the distance start to bend and sway and then you hear the whistling. Eventually it is almost a roar as your trees dip and bend next to the earth.

Here in this high valley surrounded on all sides by the mountains, the wind whips up and down and all around. A good one can blow the fire right out of your fireplace, and likewise it can feed a fire, making what was a little cheery-looking thing into a blazing hearth.

I love the wind. I love it when it rustles and whispers. And I love it when it howls and whips. But I am not silly about it. We have candles going. We know to lay in a store of fresh water. I tend to bake bread and get a soup pot going before the big storms, so we will have the comfort of homey food when the power goes. We all gravitate to the library. The dogs and cats stick close. We bring their

170

beds down and pile covers in front of the fire, where we play pinochle and Monopoly.

Because wind, like anything else, is an excuse. It can be an excuse to listen to Storm Center and be scared. To hide your eyes. It becomes an excuse to worry and fret and feel victimized by all that you cannot control. It can be another kind of excuse, too, of course. It can be the one we use to play hooky. We can hear the wind and make warm foods and snuggle in with the people we love. Sometimes no matter how well we prepare, it will cause damage. That's life. It is a story, and like every other kind of story, some people will make it horrible and some people will make it funny. There will always be the folks who choose horror films, but there will also always be people reading good character novels. Others prefer an exciting thriller. There will be mystery lovers and good-for-you-nonfiction people, too. We cannot change the way the wind blows any more than we can change the stories that happen to us. The only control we ever have is how we react to what comes, and that becomes the story we tell.

When the wind blows I want to be drinking hot thick spicy cocoa made with raw milk from the cows just up the road. It will blow. Roof tiles will fly off and every once in a while a porch will collapse. Sometimes worse. I know. It's true.

But it's not always true. Not every time.

Sometimes we will just get to miss a day of work and make fudge. You never know which one you are going to get, so you might as well stock up on the butter and chocolate chips just in case.

ooooo

The memorial service was a great success . . . as these things go.

My very dear friend Karen and her son Isaac created a wonderful slide show from photos I'd sent them. It was set to his favorite music. The first song, which you got for a while, was "You Can't

Always Get What You Want." Steve had always said he wanted that played at his funeral. He loved the Rolling Stones and this was an old favorite song. He also loved "Walk on the Wild Side" by Lou Reed. All of the kids and I remembered him singing it on various road trips. We had all sung along the refrain with him over the years.

> She said, Hey babe, take a walk on the wild side
> I said, Hey honey, take a walk on the wild side
> And the colored girls say
> Doo do doo do doo do doo do doo . . .

So that played along on the second section of the slide show. The way we set it up, the slide show played silently during the receiving line. It played across a screen to the side of one of Steve's favorite antique Windsor chairs. We had hung one of his multipocketed jackets on the back of the chair and one of his many hats was tossed in the seat. Next to it sat a table with the book that we'd found beside his bed. The book he had been reading the night before he died. His glasses were on top of that, next to a pair of binoculars from his vast collection. Also, there was a bottle of the bourbon he'd been aging, with a homemade label that had our town and his as its origin. The whole tableau looked and smelled just like him. The jacket had the whiff of Bay Rum, and the leather binocular case and fishing rods propped alongside smelled like the woods.

Our old family friend Steve Mudge had been recruited as an emcee of sorts. Steve Stimson was not a religious man, and had extracted promises at every funeral we'd ever been to together not to have a minister at his. I guess he'd always planned on dying first.

So SteveMudge,[1] who had been a lifelong friend, was recruited

---

1. Since there are several Steves in our lives, Mudge was generally SteveMudge—one word—to keep everyone straight.

to run the show. He is a master trial lawyer and knew practically everyone who would be coming. He was the perfect choice.

We'd planned that SteveMudge would open with his reminiscences after the receiving line concluded, and then he would introduce Mindy's old and very dear friend, Barb Crowder, who would read Mindy's remembrance of her brother. Benjamin had called his high school pal Greg, whose dad was a Baptist minister, and arranged for a couple of wonderful gospel singers to come. They would sing "Swing Low, Sweet Chariot," which despite its religious nature Steve had loved. He and Mindy had it sung at his mom's funeral, and he told me that day he'd like it at his.[2] Then Steve's friend Katy would give a tribute, and John would wrap it all up with the tribute from our family.

SteveMudge would offer some concluding remarks, and then the whole slide show would play, with the Rolling Stones and Lou Reed blasting.

It was in all ways lovely.

Steve's old friends from his days at Newhard Cook were there, and a bunch of his childhood pals flew in as well. His sweet second wife, Linda Rorchaste, who had been in our lives for only a short time, but who my kids all liked a lot, came, too. And Katy and their friends in the wine club from his current life. His coworkers from his current job with the State of Illinois came, and they told the story of how Steve had saved a coworker by administering CPR during a heart attack just the year before. The grateful man whose life he had saved was right there in the line. He barely had words. It was a crowded room filled with the stories of a life.

Everyone seemed to have a story that they wanted to tell Benjamin. It was amazing how many of them knew all about our kids and

---

2. In retrospect, the man had been planning his funeral for as long as I'd known him.

shook John's hand saying they had heard a lot about him. Too many times to count we heard, "Oh, and this must be Eli." Or, "Hannah, I hear you are about to graduate from Mount Holyoke."

Benjamin got wrapped in countless bear hugs as people we had never met asked if he had gotten his puppy yet. All of these people knew about us. Detailed stories about us. And if any of them thought a receiving line with one sister, one former wife, her new[3] husband, and their three kids was weird, they kept it to themselves.[4]

We'd organized a funeral dinner at Steve's favorite restaurant, but we raced off to the airport long before everyone had left. John and I had decided two days earlier that it was not too soon for us to begin Grief 101. Class had already started and we were all in it together.

We were sad and overwhelmed, but we were going to try hard to stay present and awake. John had missed a bunch of work since Steve's death. So now it was Benjamin and I who were catching that plane bound for North Carolina. He needed his mom on this trip now. Mostly, though, he needed that dog.

She had waited long enough. It was time to go get Olive.

ooooo

At four months, Olive was already too big to fly in the cabin of an airplane, and there was no way we were shipping her with the luggage. So the plan was that we would fly to North Carolina and rent a car, which we would then drive back to Vermont.

We couldn't get there early enough to pick her up on the day of the funeral, so we spent the night in Durham. We aimed to pick her up after breakfast the next day.

The breeder had four Spinones and three Irish Wolfhounds. Or maybe it was two Wolfhounds. There were a lot of big dogs, is all I

---

3. Well, after. . . not exactly new. We'd been married a good long time.

4. Cheska's notion of an Alan Alda movie kept repeating in my head.

really remember. Olive was one of two puppies left from her litter. They had planned to keep both puppies, but now the little ones were unexpectedly for sale.

We headed out to the yard where Benjamin and Olive met for the first time. It was love at first sight. They jumped, he giggled, and they both ran around with a ball. I started crying. The breeder knew about Steve's death, and she didn't seem put off by the crying. She handed me a box of Kleenex and just kept talking about dogs.

Olive was bound to become a bird hunter, and the breeder had lots of opinions that she wanted to share before we left. At least two hours went by before she seemed willing to be paid, in spite of the weeks of emails and phone calls she and Benjamin had already exchanged. Olive was hard for her to let go of. Eventually she said goodbye, feeling that her pup was in good hands with us.

North Carolina is an eleven-hour drive from Vermont. It is some seven hundred miles of mostly highway driving. That was the theory. We figured we'd take another couple of hours because of puppy stops.

But that didn't take into consideration the traffic we encountered in Virginia. It also didn't take into account a puppy that had never been on a leash before in her whole life who was now with two strangers on a long car ride. Google Maps doesn't have a setting for that.

We made plenty of puppy stops as we traveled, but the puppy didn't know what to do on them. Puppy stops are very focused activities. They have one major purpose. But Olive, excited as she was, just wouldn't get with the program. That girl would not pee. Oh, she ate. And she drank. She must have had to go. But stop though we did every hour . . . nothing. She would just walk along on the leash slightly puzzled. Apparently this driving thing was fun, but the stopping thing didn't make much sense to her. Why would we pull over? Oh well.

And I developed a headache. It started in the back of my head and wound along behind my ear down my neck. I thought at first that it was from the way I'd been sitting in the car. It was a combination of a crick in my neck and a serious headache. I was popping Motrin like candy to no effect.

I realized, naturally, that it was stress related. I occasionally get headaches and I always have medicine in my purse just in case. But somehow I had left Vermont a few days earlier with only one of those pills. Well, I had been a little distracted. And since we'd started on this trip, I'd just left the pill in my purse. I don't know, I guess I was saving it. I have no idea what I thought I was saving it for. It's not like I was thinking I should just hang on till something *really* stressful happens. But there it was in the purse doing exactly nothing for the pain. By the time I actually took the damned thing, it was way too late to do any good.

I was miserable.

Olive, the puppy that could not pee, was probably miserable, too.

And Benjamin's dad had just died, so Benjamin had to be miserable.

And with the Virginia traffic, it became clear that we were definitely not going to make it to Vermont in one day. We just were not.

So when we got to Philadelphia, I started calling hotels looking for nice places that also took dogs. I mean, sure, I could probably have found a roadside motel that we could sneak her into, but it had been a rough week. My son was grieving. Hell, I was grieving. Our puppy was . . . nonproductive. I had a headache that could peel paint off a wall. And we had been on the road for hours with our only breaks being stops where we cried about Steve and talked to a four-month-old pup about how great it would be for her to urinate. I wanted some amenities if I was staying over night. A minibar. Maybe a massage. Not a Motel 6.

Then I thought I remembered seeing doggie foods on the menu at a W Hotel once. I called Starwood, who owns those, and sure enough they take dogs. According to our GPS, there was a nice big Westin downtown, not ten minutes from where we were on the highway.

The GPS turned out to be . . . sort of . . . right. Well, had I followed it correctly it might have been completely right. I guess we'll never know for sure. An hour later, one good thing happened.

Olive peed.

Just as soon as we got out of the car as the valet held open the door. Olive let loose right there in the circular drive, underneath a lovely chandelier onto a long red carpet. Well, what did they expect? They took dogs, didn't they? And Olive knew how to make an entrance.

ooooo

This is what I had learned about grief.

Life has a way, no matter what happens, of just moving inexorably along. One minute you are looking for a pair of pants because you are bereft that your former husband has died, your current husband is writing his eulogy, and your adult children are calling you Mommy again, and then the next minute you are grinning at an otherwise inappropriately peeing puppy.[5]

It just keeps coming.

And while you don't get to pick what comes, you really do get to pick how you respond to it. That, anyway, was the theory. We intended to keep picking love and humor. The other choices were all just too bleak for words.

We eventually got back to Vermont. Benjamin and Olive

---

5. The Vermont governor has never asked me about Olive's peeing. But, to be fair, this incident happened in Pennsylvania. So I guess that explains it.

camped out at our place for a few days. A lot had happened, and we all felt like we needed to be together. Hannah was still on spring break. She'd canceled her trip so that she could be with her brother and the rest of us at the memorial service. We were all taking this last long weekend to get our bearings before going back to real life.

Then on Monday, I went to the doctor with the headache I still could not shake.

I left with a bigger one.[6]

ooooo

I'd just sat down in the exam room with my doctor.

"Hi, Doc."

"Hi, Ellen. How are you?" he replied.

"I'm well, thanks." Why do I always say that? Steve had just died, I had a headache that wouldn't quit, and I'd just driven for two days across country. Still, I started with "I'm well, thanks."

Good grief.

"Well, except we have had a bit of a rough time and I have this—"

"Hey, was that you guys last week with the fireworks?"

I hadn't come in to discuss fireworks, but one little thing I might not have mentioned about our doctor is that he lived just down the hill from us.

"Umm." I remembered John's use of the ignorance-and-clarification move. Well, why not. "Umm, possibly." Which probably would have been enough, but then I felt the need to clarify. So I might have offered a bit more than was, strictly speaking, necessary.

"A while back John drove to Pennsylvania with Eli and Timmy.

---

6. Relax, it wasn't a brain tumor. I know, you were expecting that, right? But it *was* stress. A lot of stress.

Those boys spent all of their savings on fireworks. And they discovered a new hobby in the process. They have been having a ball blowing things up ever since. Cucumbers mostly." I probably smiled. It might not have seemed as sincere as I'd planned.

"We were trying to have dinner and we were grilling outside on the first warm day of the year." He added, "We had company."

Okay. So, onward with the clarification phase.

"Oh, I'm sorry. Did they bother you?" Because, really, who could imagine the trench warfare of teenage boys with fireworks being a problem? I wondered if maybe it was time to mention the funeral we'd just had.

"The dogs kept barking over and over every time they'd set off a new one. They set off a lot."

"Shoot." I figured that I should be diplomatic. "I'm sorry. We'll ask them to use them later in the evening. Now listen, about my—"

"Aren't fireworks illegal?" he asked. Knowing the answer, of course.

"You know, I have no idea."

Well, I'm not a lawyer.

And besides, we'd just had a death in the family, for God's sake. It was a death in another state, of my former husband, who no one here knew much about, but still, a death.

"It seems to be a kid thing. You know, this *is* Vermont. There are kids shooting fireworks down at the pond all the time. I'm sorry they bothered you. We'll have them do it later in the evening so they won't interrupt dinner."

I probably could have left it there, but then it seemed that perspective was the way to go. I was wrong about that.

"It's a pretty harmless teenage diversion, you know? And it's usually only about fifteen minutes. Now listen, the reason I am here—"

"Well, Ellen, I am pretty sure they are illegal, and they make the dogs bark."

Well then.

"We like to have dinner out on the terrace and when summer comes we will be doing it more."

And I liked to see a doctor who let me finish a sentence, and I wished my kid's dad hadn't just died, and I really wished we could do something about my headache, but it's an imperfect world.

"Okay, fine. Can I please talk about why I am here now? You know, my health?"

He seemed a little surprised that the conversation would turn in that direction. In a doctor's office.

"Oh, sure. Sorry," he muttered.

"Okay, so—"

"Do you intend to put a stop to the fireworks, though?"

"You know . . . you know . . . oh, hell. No, I am probably not."

I used to ask a doctor where he or she studied. Sometimes I'd ask about their philosophy of medicine. Maybe how they treat the antibiotic question, or whether they explore alternative medicine when a patient is interested. But since it was pretty clear I was going to have to be shopping for a new doctor very soon, I mentally amended my list of questions.

I would now ask where they lived.

Because Vermont is really tiny, and my kid likes fireworks.[7]

ooooo

I grew up terrified of fireworks. I had heard all the awful stories of kids who put their eyes out . . . lost fingers . . . caught themselves

---

7. He did fix my headaches though. He is actually a great diagnostician, a really good doc. He just doesn't like fireworks. Who could blame him?

on fire. I mean, really, who gives explosives to a kid . . . for fun? Certainly, my kids would never shoot fireworks. What kind of parents would permit such a thing? How did those kids get a hold of fireworks, anyway?

Then I met Eli. And Timmy.

Timmy has big brothers. And big brothers have firecrackers. That was just the beginning. Eli would come home from Timmy's house all keyed up and excited with a pocketful of firecrackers of his own.

Pretty soon he moved on to bottle rockets. There would be mounds of dirt in our yard, and then giant explosions that would send dirt spraying in a raucous din. I hated to be a killjoy. I mean, I love a good explosion just like the next guy. But this all seemed awfully dangerous.

I didn't understand everything about the firecracker appeal, but what I did understand was that boys needed to learn to take risks. All kids do, of course, but I think boys most especially. They have all that propelling testosterone, and they aren't working it off in the same ways as they had for thousands of years. We didn't live on a real farm. We weren't sending him off to the battlefield at thirteen.

Sports help. But sports just don't take up enough time. So in modern society, some boys get into trouble a lot. Beer and cigarettes are the least of it. I figured that the boys in our world needed risk if they were to avoid the trouble spots. Measured risk. But risk.

As a result, all of our friends had been treated to fireworks displays. And no birds flew within a hundred feet of the house. Our airspace was filled with smoke.

So when the guy on the phone said "Officer" I immediately wondered what Eli had blown up. I mean really. We'd just had a funeral and I was a little off my game. What now?

ooooo

The phone was ringing and I absent-mindedly answered.

"Hello."

"Hello, this is Officer *Wah-wah-wah-wah wah wah wah.*"

After "Officer" my hearing began to fail. I might as well have been Charlie Brown. I couldn't make out what the fellow was saying. I immediately had my own questions, though.

Where is Eli? was high on the list.

What has he blown up now? was a close second.

Last fall it had been a bunch of pumpkins down on the green. I admit that I didn't really feel like blowing up a pumpkin myself, but it seemed safe enough for them to do it. Only, there was pumpkin all down the street the next day. And it hadn't rained in weeks. So there may have been a bit of a smell. Our phone rang all weekend after that one. It had been hard to get a long-enough hose.

One village neighbor had very kindly threatened to call the FBI.

"This is how terrorists get their start" were her exact words, I think.

I wondered, too, where Benjamin was.

God, I hoped he still had David Silver's phone number with him. David is our friend, but he also happens to be a criminal defense lawyer. All my kids have his cell phone number in their wallets. Because, you know, you just never know.

Officer? Good grief. What could it be this time?

I tried to listen harder.

"Is Oscar your dog, ma'am?"

Oscar? Not Eli. Not Benjamin. Oscar?

Oh. Oscarrrrr.

"Yes, sorry. Oscar? Oscar! Here, boy. Where are you?" As if my calling out to the dog would make him appear. Especially since I knew he wouldn't. Still, it was worth a try.

"Ma'am, I have him." Officer Charlie Brown's Teacher was pretty sure the suspect was in custody.

"I am down here at the inn. We came in to Vermont to see the leaves. Boy, you guys sure live in a pretty spot up here. Anyway, your dog wandered into our room."

Oh, right.

He was calling about Oscar. So apparently Oscar had gone visiting. At least it wasn't Olive. She might have peed on him.

"Uh, which inn?" I ventured. Well, I had to be sure.

"The Dorset Inn. I am sitting out on the porch with him now. I gave him a little sausage. I hope that's okay. He's a great guy."

So we didn't have a kid in jail or having blown anything up. This guy wasn't even from here. I guess he must just be identified as "officer" wherever he was from. And Oscar was missing? Someone must have left a door open. Oscar had a thing about open doors. We had escaped doom. No one had been arrested. Well, not this time, anyway.

"On my way."

ooooo

Oscar had friends all over town. He had this terrible habit of racing through an open door with his head down. He is sort of a furry linebacker. He couldn't hear when he was tucked and racing. We nicknamed him the Gingerbread Man, because he was so fast that you could barely see it while it was happening. We knew where he usually went, so we could follow a few minutes behind.

Jim at Barrows House would point in the "which way did he go" universal answer and we would keep going. Oscar sometimes stopped in at a neighbor's who had recently lost a dear old dog. He would head straight for the toy basket and fetch the ball for a while, before the neighbor got around to calling us. Other days, he would wander down into the village and walk into unsuspecting people's houses for a look around. We would be out looking for him and pretty soon someone would call. Oscar was having ice cream with friends.

These runs were scary, because since Oscar was so social, he headed down to the village instead of running the other way, into the woods. The woods would have been fine. Route 30 is between our house and the village down at the bottom of the hill. So that scared us to death.

We were practicing dog-calming techniques all the time now. Our appliance-repair guy had suggested a shock collar. I couldn't imagine that on this sweetest of dogs. But he was a runner.

Some folks had suggested an electric fence. We had a real fence over about half an acre. The fence wasn't the problem. The door was. That wasn't quite right, either. It was Oscar. Not the door.

Oscar is a Wheaten Terrier, a Gund toy come to life. He is the most loving creature. And he makes some very soulful eye contact with those long-lashed flirty eyes of his. No matter where he was when we finally caught up to him . . . a neighbor's house . . . Manchester . . . Timbuktu . . . he would run over and hop in the car. He seemed to be equally laughing with us and licking us. He seemed gleefully surprised every single time. He'd hop in and lick our faces as if to say, "Wow, how cool is this! You guys come here, too!"

I loved this boy, but the running thing . . . well, we were working on it.

When I picked up Oscar at the Dorset Inn, Officer Wah-Wah-Wah said, "That dog of yours is a saint." Weirdly, we'd heard this same word used about him several times and from lots of different people.

He explained. "My wife broke her ankle on this trip. She got it set at the hospital yesterday. We would just go home, but we are meeting our daughter here soon. She's coming home from Europe from her honeymoon."

Reaching down to rub Oscar behind the ear, he continued. "If we don't see our daughter this week, we might not see her for another year. They are going to live in California, where her husband is in medical school. So my wife is pretty miserable. She can't get comfortable enough to sleep."

Looking down at my dog, he said, "But your guy? He came here, smelled her cast, and sat quietly beside her with his head on her knee. It was a funny thing, but while she petted him she finally fell sound asleep. He just sat very still. Like a little fuzzy saint."

Saint Oscar.

I wondered if his new cousin Olive could teach him about doors.

ooooo

UNDERNEATH

I like listening to dog owners who say their dogs never beg at the table. Those owners never feed the dog "human food."

"If you feed them, they will beg." It is prevailing wisdom among a certain kind of pet owner.

I always wonder what exactly they mean by human food. I guess they mean their dogs get only kibble. But a quick scan of the ingredients of most of the good dog foods reveals lots of foods that would be familiar to us . . . chicken, salmon, carrots, beets.

Human food.

Granted, it's human food that's crushed into a generally tasteless, smelly brown kibble. When I read those bags, it always strikes me that a lifetime of eating kibble is not what nature intended. Dogs need and desire a varied diet just like we do. Would you want to eat the same damn thing day after day, year after year?

Me neither.

On the other side of the debate are the ardent raw-diet pet owners. They fix up big bowls of beef, chicken, green beans, and apples, and spend a huge amount of time doing it. There are countless websites and books dedicated to the glories of natural dog diets. But I can never quite manage to give over such a hunk of time to the preparation of pet meals. With three dogs, one cat, and twelve chickens, I can imagine that would be a full-time occupation. Throw in the kids and adults at our table and I would need a staff the size of Downton's just to manage the meals.

So our dogs get table scraps. They get carrots shaved on their kibble, and they get bits of beef or chicken or scrambled eggs. And sometimes I am not disciplined enough to put it all into their bowls in the kitchen. Sometimes I share with them . . . from . . . well, you know, the table. Violet especially loves this about me.

I know I shouldn't.

Or maybe I just suspect I shouldn't. I guess I am not convinced.

John and I are what the pet books euphemistically call permissives.[1] But the dogs surely love it. And it turns out, I love having a warm dog snuggled on top of my feet under the table. Our dogs don't hang out with their heads on the table. Really they more . . . lurk. Underneath. They are hopeful, and that hope is often rewarded. Sometimes we take the scraps to the kitchen and feed them where we suppose we should. Sometimes we don't.

So at dinner parties under the big fancy table there are usually dogs. Sometimes they put a warm chin on a friendly lap. Usually they stretch out across feet. I prefer to think of them as furry foot warmers, not begging pets.

And we love to take them out to outdoor restaurants too. Our dogs are as much a part of the café set as the rest of us.

During parties they are well behaved. Our guys know not to grab a tenderloin sandwich off a low table. They keep their noses out of the guacamole. Oh, maybe every once in a while something gets swiped. But, you know, they're like a pickpocket: fast and stealthy. Guests barely notice the dogs after the first five minutes.

So dogs at the table. Well. Yes.

I guess we always make room for them, too.

ooooo

---

1. Those authors should see how we parent our kids.

CHAPTER NINE

Bad Juju

A FEW DAYS AFTER WE GOT HOME FROM NORTH CAROLINA, Benjamin got a box in our mail. He lived on his own now, but from time to time we still got mail for him. This package was about eight inches by twelve inches and maybe six inches high. When we were back in St. Louis, we had taken a few things out of Steve's house and stashed them at Mindy's. We wanted to come back and look at them later, but didn't want to leave them in the house. So there was a pretty good chance that this might have been all those watches that we had put aside. Or it could have been some of Steve's small personal items that Benjamin had an attachment to. It might have been anything.

It wasn't.

Benjamin tore into the box hoping that Mindy had sent the watch with the big yellow dial. He'd always liked that one.

"Do you guys have a knife? God, she packed this tight," he said.

"Honey, your dad used to say that Aunt Mindy should have stock in Scotch tape. She loves to wrap, and by golly nothing is coming undone under her watch," I replied. "There will probably be aluminum foil in there, too. She loves anything shiny. Here."

I handed him the pair of kitchen scissors.

"No foil, but it seems like this whole thing is encased in plastic. Why would she do that?" He was hacking away without much luck. "I really need a knife. I hope she put his pocketknives in here, too. 'Course, I may never get it open to see."

Plastic wrap?

That seemed excessive even for Mindy. Still, I guess if she wanted to make sure it was waterproof she might try plastic wrap. You wouldn't want watches to get wet, though God knows that Steve would have made sure you could submerge the damned things to ten thousand feet or something. Still, she'd never plastic-wrapped anything for us.

"This is really heavy," Benjamin added. "Do you think she threw in that trout book I left on the counter? SteveMudge told me all about that one. Steve had lent it to him a while ago."

He rustled and tugged and poked at that damned package. It was almost fighting him.

"I meant to take it to read on the plane. I hope that's in here. You don't remember the name of that author do you? Aha! Got it . . ."

And he did, too. I knew before he said a word. He was backing away from the opened box on our counter.

"It's from the funeral home," he flatly said.

"Oh. Sure. I see." And I did. We'd sort of forgotten to expect this. I needlessly added, "It's your dad's ashes."

I looked at him. He was shaking his head and heading out the door.

"I don't want 'em. You keep 'em."

"Okay, honey. I will." We were talking from separate rooms, but I added that "We should probably start to think about when we want to scatter them, though."

We had originally looked up a place near Steve's home called Carpenter Road before the memorial service. We'd found the map, and figured out where it was. Steve liked to take long meandering summer drives on that country road to look at the stars through his various optical instruments. The kids had all been out there to watch meteor showers, and it was a place he had loved. It wasn't too far away, and we thought maybe after the service we would all take a drive together and scatter them to the wind. Only, the time got away from us. People stayed in line telling us stories for a long time, and then there was the funeral dinner. That meant lots more conversation. Then we had to hustle out to get to the airport in time to pick up Olive. Finally, we'd just asked the funeral home to ship them to us. We'd planned to figure it out later.

Later had come.

Steve was sitting on my kitchen counter.

He'd never done that before.

He'd never fit in an eight-by-twelve box, either.

Hmm.

Benjamin said, "I've already been thinking about it. How about the river where we fished?"

I followed him into the mud room. "That's a great idea. Do you wanna do it this weekend?" I added hopefully. I mean, it seemed the sort of thing to work out.

"Umm. No. Uh . . . I want to wait," he said uncomfortably. "Look, I have got to go. I have a client meeting in an hour."

He lowered his face for a quick kiss on the cheek and was gone.

I got it. I could understand wanting to wait. Scattering the ashes had a new air of finality about it. Losing his dad had been a shock. He needed time to adjust. We'd just wait until he brought it up. There was no rush.

Only, in the meantime, what was I supposed to do with Steve?

ooooo

Almost as soon as Benjamin was out of the driveway the dogs started barking. This happens when you have a pack of three. One of them sounds the alarm. Pippi, usually.

Pippi is a Moodle. Okay, so I think she's officially a Maltipoo:

half Poodle and half Maltese. But our friends Ellen and Roger have one, too,[1] and they thought that "Maltipoo" was just a little too . . . precious . . . so, they'd come up with "Moodle." It fit. And Pippi the Moodle barks.

It's just who she is. For Pippi, cars in the driveway, dogs on the trail, kids kicking off snowshoes in the mudroom are all cause for a cheery little barking session. She barks, therefore she is.

Violet will sometimes set off the cavalcade, though. Violet is our Bernese Mountain Dog. She is an elegant young lady, and barking is not really her style these days. She is a fraidy cat of a dog, though. Everything scares her the first time she comes across it. Vacuum cleaners, kids on sleds, basketballs. Everything. When she was about nine months old, she barked to illustrate her worry. So, the round of barking could be her fault. Thankfully she had grown out of the overbarking, and now only the threat of an "intruder" caused the occasional deep, loud warning.

And Oscar? Well, Oscar is glad to join in with the occasional howl. He's a social sort of dog. So if a howl is going on . . . well, Oscar is glad to take up the slack.

Right then they were all announcing something big.

I went to the door.

It was Ernie. And a woman I hadn't met. More importantly, Ernie was with a woman that the dogs hadn't met.

"Hi, Ellen. I'd like you to meet my wife."

Ernie is our appliance-repair guy. Some people have lawyers on retainer. We have repairmen. Neither John nor I is very handy. Ernie keeps the dishwasher, clothes dryer, stove, and fridge in good repair. He's competent and cheerful. Plus, he loves our dogs. He

---

1. Milo.

was practically perfect. So normally he just walked right in.[2] This knocking business was new. In fact, now that I noticed, he wasn't in his work clothes.

"Sorry to bother you, Ellen, but I wanted to introduce my wife to Violet. See, we just had a really sad thing happen and—" He was choked up and it took a minute.

"Well, we are thinking of getting a Berner. So we thought we'd meet Violet."

"Oh, no, Ernie. I am so sorry." Ernie was upset, and clearly so was his wife.

"Yes, we uh, we lost our lab," he continued. "He was my wife's best buddy. I thought . . . well, can we come in?"

"Oh, God. Oh, of course," I blurted. I'd kind of forgotten we were just standing in the doorway with the dogs howling. I looked at his wife and tried to welcome her. "Hi, I'm Ellen. Come on in. Violet's right here. You will love her. She's calm and quiet, most of the time, and she has an enormous vocabulary."

I was giving the postcard-sized Berner story as Ernie's wife laid her purse down on the counter. We'd had Berners since we lived in St. Louis. Our first, Eloise, was so great that she had sold us on the breed ever since. They are smart, beautiful, and wonderful companions for families. Our Violet was a great in-front-of-the-fire-in-the-library dog. She could certainly comfort these poor grieving folks. Grieving . . .

Oh shit, the ashes.

Ernie's wife was laying her purse right on the counter. Next to Steve.

---

2. Okay, I admit it. We don't lock our doors. One of us is always here. Anyway, it's Vermont. A crime wave would take us all out. Not locking your doors is kind of a state tradition. I don't even own a key to this house. At the closing I asked and the realtor just shrugged. Fine by me.

Well, that's all she needs, to see someone's ashes while she is newly in mourning herself.

I . . . well, I sort of blurted . . . maybe barked, "Here, let me just get that box out of your way." I snatched up the box and stepped toward the library. It was heavy. Heavier than I'd expected. Where to put it? Well. That's not something I've ever had to think about before. I stood there looking around. Then I looked down at the big, heavy, ugly box. It's not just every day that you have to think about what to do with your former husband's ashes. This was a mildly surreal puzzle.

The box wasn't pretty enough to sit out on a shelf . . . you know, decoratively, and besides, there was kind of an eww factor. I walked into the dining room, which we only use a few times a month, and stuck him on the sideboard for safekeeping. I figured I'd think about it later.

Only, after Ernie and his wife left, I forgot all about it.

Well, until the dinner party that Saturday.

ooooo

I was digging around looking for my blue table runner when I saw the box. It had become sort of invisible to me all week, but it wasn't really invisible. I mean, *really* not invisible. It was the sort of thing that guests would notice. And, you know, that's a conversation that couldn't go well.

"Ellen, what a lovely dining room you have. And that hefty cardboard box marked "Remains" goes so well with the scorched-table aesthetic you've created here." They might offer.

I would, of course, reply, "Oh, right. That's Steve. Well, Steve's ashes, anyway."

"Oh, really? And who's Steve?"

"Well, Steve . . . Steve is my . . . well, was my . . . husband.

Well, ex . . . er . . . former husband. Like, really former. You know, like twenty-five-years former. Oh, and dead, so I guess *former* former husband, at that. He just died, you see. And we haven't quite figured out what to do with him yet. Why do you ask?"

Did I mention that our guests were clients? And one of the guests was a new client, besides. I could just see myself trying to explain why I had my ex-husband's ashes in the dining room. Just a side note: if you are trying to figure out the best way to explain what your ex-husband's ashes are doing on the sideboard, then you might want to ask yourself just what you are, in fact, doing with your ex-husband's ashes on the sideboard.

They wouldn't be too out of bounds thinking maybe I had killed him.

I could already picture John gently raising his eyebrows and giving that slight smile of his that says, "Ellen, where are you going here?"

Truth is, I had no idea. But I did know that this could not possibly be good for business.

I needed to move Steve.

But, you know, back to square one. Where?

And then, of course, the dogs started barking, again. Touch the box and three dogs howling. It was like a damned game show.

I went to the door.

Keith Weber, our oil guy. Our kids went to school together. He is the sweetest guy in the world. And, well, he likes to chat. One thing led to another, as it always does around here, and Steve stayed where he was on the sideboard, till about an hour before the party.

It wasn't like I didn't think about it.

But what the hell do you do about this? I mean, I couldn't put him out just anywhere. I mean, he's not exactly a lovely centerpiece.

I guess he could be a conversation piece, but I didn't think he would match the library décor. I suppose I could put him in the bathroom tub. He certainly loved that Jacuzzi. And, you know, I guessed he was probably naked in that box. But that's not something you want to explain to a guest who asks for the bathroom.

"Oh, don't mind Steve, he's not shy. Just don't turn on the faucet."

No, that wouldn't do.

And I couldn't just stick him in the basement. "Basement" is a generous term, really. "Cellar" is better. "Dungeon" is a little strong. "Cave" is probably closer. It's pretty awful down there. I couldn't just shove him in there.

So, not the basement.

By the time the dogs started barking to tell me the guests had arrived, I still hadn't found a place. So in a fit of desperation, I grabbed him—well, the box—and stuck it up high in our utility closet. With the mops and vacuum and cleaning supplies.

I know. I know.

It was not perfect. But, then, maybe you can tell me just what the hell is?

ooooo

For weeks, he sat there.

I know. Weeks.

Every time I would open the door to grab the vacuum or get a hammer, there he was. I could just hear him. "Ellen, for God's sakes. This is really not suitable. Would I stick you in an old closet? Come on, now."

He would have had a point. I guess after all these years, I could carry on both sides of the conversation. Not surprising, really.

But here we were. Benjamin had said not one more word about the ashes for ages. Just last weekend, I'd tried again.

"Hon, I have been thinking about your dad's ashes . . ." I started.

"Oh, Mom. Not this again! Really, can't it wait?" I really wasn't pestering him, but I did think we should do something. Benjamin went on that he "was thinking we should have Aunt Mindy here when we do it. Maybe SteveMudge, too. But I just can't think about it right now, all right? Olive and I are meeting the trainer this afternoon. Dogs pick up on your emotions. I do not want to be all worked up about the ashes when she and I are working together in the woods, huh?"

Well, that was reasonable. Mindy should come.

"Oh, sweetie. I'm sorry. We can wait as long as you want. Of course we can. And having Aunt Mindy and SteveMudge is a good idea."

I figured that since we had a bit of planning started I could wedge some more in. "I could have a little dinner party with our Vermont friends and we could have sort of a mini-memorial for him here if you want. In fact . . ."

"*Mo-mmm!*"

"Oh, right. Sorry. Sorry. It's just that I worry about those ashes. But, I'm sorry, hon. Take as long as you need."

He gave me that what's-wrong-with-you-crazy-woman? look that he'd honed as a teenager. "Worry about the ashes?! They aren't going anywhere. It's not like it's really him. Come on, Mom. God."

He was right, of course. But then, he didn't know I had Steve in the utility closet, either. I wondered if that would change the equation any.

Okay, so I just needed to forget about the closet. This was Benjamin's dad, and so, in a very real sense, it was his journey. Not mine.

But here's the thing, if it was his journey then why did I have to have the goddamned ashes? In a closet. Next to the Swiffer.

ooooo

There is a long narrow shelf just a bit higher than the door when you open the utility closet. It is the width of the closet but not very deep. This closet is built behind a staircase, so it slopes just a few feet in. And this particular shelf was where we kept odds and ends. Small odds and ends. The draft blockers, for example. You know, those long cloth-things that block drafts through the bottom of the door during the winter. I think there were a couple of pots from kitchen-window plants that had died. And Steve.

He was right. It really wasn't suitable. Besides, I opened that closet all the time. The Resolve was in there. When you have three dogs and your son brings his puppy over all the time, the rugs get a workout. So I was constantly reaching in there for the Resolve, or that little tube-thingy that takes out watermarks.[3] And, there was Steve.

His picture might as well have been on that box. And it was not a happy picture, either. His face was all scrunched up, and he was complaining. What's worse is that I knew he was right.

Or, he would have been if he'd been alive. Which he wasn't. I knew that. I was not losing my mind.

Okay, maybe just a teensy bit. But it was those damned ashes. Look, just try putting your old . . . ex . . . former husband's ashes on a shelf in a cramped closet, and see if it doesn't make you a little weird.-er.

One day I mentioned all of this to my friend Ellen. She was calling to see how Benjamin was doing. But what she got was my little ash problem instead.

---

3. Tibet Almond Sticks. Amazing product. You just rub it into the ring or scratch or whatever, and voila. It's like it was never there. With a bunch of messy people and an antiques-filled house, this stuff is a must.

"I don't know, I mean he loves that dog. I think she is saving his life. Well, that and the fishing. He loved fishing last year, but this year he is going crazy over it. He stops at rivers and streams all over the place and throws his dad's line in the water. And have you seen his Facebook? It's wild all the fish he's catching. It's a good thing he's a catch-and-release guy or I am telling you Vermont would run out of fish. But, Ellen, he won't even talk about sprinkling his dad's ashes. Not a word."

I'm not sure I breathed. It just sort of rushed out of me in one long gush.

My friend Ellen was a therapist in her recent past, and somehow, telling her about a problem is almost enough to make it go away. First of all, she is brilliant. And she is a calm, rational pragmatist to boot. She can do a little therapy magic, and when she talks to you it's warm honey poured directly on your soul. She's also a decent shot with a Winchester, but I didn't need that skill just at the moment. Just the soothing talk.

"He will when he's ready, hon. You guys are doing everything right." Well, clearly she knew what I needed to hear. "I think the fishing and the puppy are wonderful diversions. He knows you will be ready to scatter those ashes whenever he says that he is ready. He trusts you to help him carry this burden in the meantime."

See? Smart and comforting. But . . .

"Okay, I know. I know. But Ellen, listen . . . he is making me keep the ashes! And I have nowhere to put them. I mean, I can't leave them out, can I? And I feel guilty for stuffing them away. And please don't tell anyone this but . . . I have him in my utility closet! And every single time I go in there I can just hear him yelling at me to get him out. Well, not actually yelling. I mean, I am not hearing voices. I am not crazy. Exactly. Or, not really."

I wanted to be very clear about that part. It's an important part.

"But I can imagine it. Because, you know, no one would want

to be in a utility closet. Not even Steve. Not even a dead Steve. I do know he's dead. I do. But I still can't shake the feeling that he'd have a fucking preference."

I took a breath. We were both quiet for a second. In fact, several seconds. Long enough that I started to wonder . . .

"Ellen? Are you still there . . . ?"

And then with the voice of compassion, reason, years of experience, a PhD, and a license to carry a rifle in the Vermont backwoods, my friend Ellen said, "Hon. Those ashes are bad juju!"

So much for calm and rational.

○○○○○

Lyndee lived in New York State, just over the Vermont border, with her five dogs. Benjamin had heard of her from one of the Spinone breeders when he'd been looking for Olive. He wanted Olive to be a hunting dog, but none of us knew anything at all abut training a hunting dog.

We'd read everything we could get our hands on about it, and it seemed that hiring a trainer was the best way to go if you wanted her to hunt. Even that was fraught, though. Some trainers take your dog away from you for six weeks. That felt completely wrong to us. You and your puppy need to bond to one another. Olive didn't need a stranger in her life in that way.

In addition to the isolation, many hunters were using shock collars. Benjamin was pretty sure he was against this. I was positive that I was.

"But Mom," he reasoned. "We really don't know anything about hunting. Bob has never had a dog. He just hires guides. What if this is the only way to keep the dogs really safe?"

I didn't know anything at all about hunting. That much was true. But I did know about dogs. Now, it's true that mine were trained in only the very loosest sense. John and I were . . . permissive.

Our dog owning was a lot like our parenting. You love the dogs up, meet them where they are, and have a couple of things which you simply do not allow. Everything else is up for discussion.

And our dogs were well behaved. Well, mostly. They were incredibly well socialized. They loved other dogs and people. We made sure they were well exercised and never bored. They could be left alone. They didn't chew, bark excessively,[4] or grab food off the counters.

You know, we could have a party with food sitting out everywhere, and other than a few plaintive looks at "weak" guests, they knew how to act. Mostly. But the idea of shock collars appalled me.

And while I didn't know anything about hunting, luckily I had always been a good debater. So I countered, "Look, there have been hunters a lot longer than there have been shock collars. What did they do before?"

Point Mom.

Then he found Lyndee. She organized outings every Saturday morning. And there were no shock collars, either. A bunch of hunters would come work their dogs together in the woods around her house. In this way, Benjamin met many other hunters and other dogs. He saw a wide variety of training techniques.

Eventually, he and Lyndee set up a few outings for one-on-one instruction. Lyndee was a hunter with a wild, cheery, unruly pack. They weren't trained within an inch of their lives, but they all knew how to flush and retrieve. They were a loving bunch who lived closely with her in her house, just like ours did with us. This woman knew her away around hunting and around hunting dogs. Olive loved her. The first time Olive pointed, Benjamin and Lyndee practically had a party. And the day she pointed her first grouse, we really had a party.

---

4. Much.

We had been to the pet store that day for new dog bones, and we were already grilling steaks for Will and Eli when Benjamin called to tell us. We invited him to come over right away.

We gave Olive her bone as soon as she came in the door. We were all petting and congratulating her. She seemed very sure this party was about her.

"You should have seen it," Benjamin enthused. "She pointed beautifully. It was amazing. Then she tiptoed silently right up to the bird. I couldn't believe how close she got when he flew up."

There was a lot of pride in those eyes. "Wow. It was fantastic." He looked over at that dog with paternal pride and told her, "You are the best girl in the whole world, Olive."

"Yay, Olive!" I said. "What a good girl. Where's the bird?"

"No bird," Benjamin explained. "Her daddy can't shoot worth shit. But she can sure point, can't you, Olive!"

ooooo

It wasn't long before the pictures started showing up on Facebook. There would be Olive with a bird in her mouth next to a pile of feathered corpses on the ground. No Vermont bird was safe.

You could call "Come around!" and Olive, from a quarter-mile away, would come bounding through the woods. She'd be heeling at your side before you could count to ten. This dog was trained. She heels. She points. And when her daddy gets the shot, she retrieves like a master.

It got so you never saw one of them without the other. They were inseparable. Olive went on every film shoot with Benjamin. Along the way, they'd pull over and run into the woods when the cover looked right for a quick little hunt. They hunted three or four times a week. She didn't need a leash no matter the conditions: busy farmers' market or deep woods. Olive was a perfect companion. And growing, too. Benjamin had gotten her a big dog bed, which was on the floor right next to his. He was reading all of the training books, and through trial and error he had found his own style. Every night they'd go to bed. He'd climb into his bed, and Olive would curl up in her dog bed. It was sweet. Of course, she might have wanted to try out his bed, too, but there were rules. He was very clear with us about all the rules. But, as the days got shorter, they both had secretly discovered . . . compromise.

I stopped by one very early morning to leave a plate of cookies on the counter. I was on my way to one of my client's for an early breakfast, and I passed right by Benjamin's house on the way. We'd baked cookies the night before, and I thought I would just sneak in and leave them as a surprise for him.

It was awfully quiet in there. I wondered if Olive was on her bed, so I tiptoed into the living room and peeked around the door into his bedroom. Her bed was there all right . . . empty. That's because she was stretched out behind his back. Boy, she had gotten tall. I think they were actually spooning. So much for all those rules.

○○○○○

October was their favorite month. Or maybe it was just Benjamin's favorite month. It was hard not to generalize around these two.[5] October is when grouse season opens but fly-fishing season hasn't closed.

"Mom, today is my favorite day of the year. I can hunt and fish on the same day. And for the next month! I've got this damned new client, though, which is really gonna get in the way. I wonder if I could close up shop in October . . . ?"

"Benjamin!"

---

5. I was beginning to wonder how I would ever get grandkids now. I mean, what were the odds of him meeting a wife out in the woods with his dog?

"Come on, I'm kidding here. You know I am *such* a kidder . . . but, just October. It's a thought."

A few weeks after Steve died, John and Benjamin had flown to St. Louis to pack up his house. They'd rented one of those pods to ship to Vermont and filled it with everything Benjamin wanted to keep. They'd arranged for a local auctioneer to manage the rest. Steve was a lifelong collector, so it wound up being three auctions. It was a lot of stuff. Still, Benjamin came back with an awful lot of stuff.

It turned out that every single time Steve had ever bought a fly rod for the last twenty-odd years, he had bought two. One for him and one for Benjamin. He had apparently been planning on this all of Benjamin's life.

And no one knew.

Now those rods were getting a ton of use. It wasn't long before outdoor companies were picking up Benjamin's photos off of Facebook. There was one where Olive was standing proudly with a bird in her mouth, and at her feet was a gun next to a fly rod in shallow water with a rainbow trout waiting to be set free. Benjamin was living in the woods, running that dog, and now even getting paid a bit for the privilege. There are worse ways to deal with loss.

In this way time passed, and Benjamin grieved. He and Olive were paying tribute to Steve in the woods and streams around Vermont. It was really quite beautiful in its own way. A little bloody . . . but beautiful.

Meanwhile, here was still the problem in my closet.

"Benjamin, we have got to do something with these ashes . . . hon."

"Hon" can cover a multitude of emotions . . . sins . . . and challenges. So I deployed "hon" with earnestness. It seemed to work.

"I know," he replied.

"I mean it. Either we have got to scatter them, or you have to take them. He can't stay here any longer." I did *not* say "live here." That would have been wrong.

"Look, I said I know." He said with some exasperation.

"Yes, I hear you. And I am trying to be sweet about this. I have been really patient. But it has been a whole year." And it had. A year of avoiding . . . I don't know . . . not eye contact . . . I guess box contact.

"Mom, it's just a box," he countered. As if he actually believed that. If it was "just a box" it wouldn't have still been in my house. We would have dealt with it already. He knew it wasn't "just a box," but still. It. Had. Been. A. Year.

Besides, he had no idea what was really going on with The Box.

The previous Saturday we had been cleaning out the basement and the attic. We'd rented a dumpster so that we could make a good job of it. And we'd filled that monster in three days. Filled.

I was sick of all the clutter around the house. That little house at the pond that we rented in the summer had no clutter. None. And when we'd gotten back, I'd felt overwhelmed. Okay, so it wasn't just the clutter. I had a client who was driving me crazy. But my house was full of too much stuff as well. And I was getting fatter again too from all the work stress. And my ex-husband was in a box in my closet next to the Resolve.

I mean, there were factors. But I figured I could at least manage the damned clutter. Why did we keep all this stuff, anyway? There was a beautiful, but broken, wrought iron table in the basement. Our repair guy had tried and failed and failed to fix it. I'd even taken it to a restorer. Well, okay, it wasn't exactly a furniture restorer. It was a car body shop, but still. They restore metal things. Anyway, I kept thinking one of these days I would find the perfect guy with the perfect tool who would finally fix it for me. Meanwhile, that broken table took up a bunch of space that I needed. So no more, I say! Into the dumpster it went, along with all manner of other broken, old, useless stuff.

We ended up getting a second dumpster after filling the first all the way up. We filled that one too. I managed to lose five thousand pounds in less than a week. It was the most successful diet I had ever been on.

The only trouble had been Steve.

When we got to the utility closet, I made a pile. Ratty bucket? Out.

Big plastic bin with broken lid, the one that always had to have something on top of it to keep it closed, which was usually the ratty bucket? Gone.

Steve. Okay, he had to go back in I guessed.

Half an hour later, I was putting the closet back to rights, arranging the tools, putting all the cleaning supplies in a cute basket, and feeling quite smug. Until I couldn't find Steve.

He wasn't on the shelf.

Shit. Where was he?

I tend to misplace things, so I figured I'd just carried him absentmindedly into the kitchen or something. Maybe I'd put him under the sink.

No.

Huh.

I looked in the dining room. Maybe I'd thought the sideboard was missing him. Besides, I had been washing all of the linens that we kept in the buffet. Maybe I'd carried him in there.

Nope.

I looked in the buffet and on all of the chairs. Where the hell was he, anyway?

After another day of searching, I knew I was going to have to face it. I must have accidentally carried him out to the dumpster.

Shitshitshit.

I certainly didn't want to tell Benjamin, of course. I imagined that I could always make a box of fireplace ashes, if it came to that.

And, I *really* didn't want to tell John.

I mean, this was just beyond the pale. I couldn't imagine how I was going to ask my husband if he would mind dumpster-diving for his wife's ex-husband's ashes.

That was more than I could ask.

Besides, I could manage this. It's not like we had thrown garbage in there or anything.

The dumpster was too tall for me to see over, so I carried a chair outside and climbed up to peer in. Right away, I wondered why we had thrown away my grandmother's old afghan. I quickly realized that John had never liked it, that was why. It was moth-eaten and shabby. But still. Well, that wasn't very nice. Hmm.

I was determined that Grandma's afghan was coming back inside. The deal was we were supposed to agree on what went in, and I certainly did not remember agreeing to this! And, hey, weren't those the rolls of wallpaper that matched the paper in our vestibule? What the hell?

Three hours later, I had brought back in . . . possibly . . . a hundred pounds of stuff.[6] And Steve. He'd been there, all right. In the dog-food bin.

Whoops.

We simply had to do something about these ashes.

○○○○○

Finally, SteveMudge was coming to fish. Hooray and hallelujah! He had a trip to make to New York City, and we were scheduled for a visit on his way home to St. Louis. The whole trip came to us on too short notice to get Mindy to come, but we could set aside some of the ashes for when she came . . . or something.

---

6. Or priceless treasures that my husband had cruelly chucked out of our lives without me knowing it. But probably just stuff.

In Benjamin's house. Not mine. No way.

Not in my closet.

It was time to scatter at last.

I went to an antiques shop and bought some beautiful silver containers for the ashes. It seemed wrong to just pour him out of a box. I somehow thought that a silver container was important. Now that he was out of the closet. And the dumpster. I had a beautiful silver pitcher at home, but that didn't seem quite right for this. Plus, then I would never want to use it again. You just can't pour iced tea out of a pitcher you used to scatter your ex-husband's ashes from.

So anyway, I bought two little vessels. Neither turned out to be big enough. This man made a lot of damned ashes. I guess he had always been a big guy. But really, this was ridiculous. You'd think that after moving him around every room in my house I would have a pretty good idea how large a container to use. Oh, well, I went back for one more.

Truth is, he didn't quite fit in that one, either. So I divided him into all three. And then I tossed out the box. But then, in the middle of the night, I felt guilty about tossing that box out in the trash. What if there was ash left in the bottom? Had I really gotten all of it out? Well, that was Steve in there. Sort of. He'd already spent a year in a closet. Could I really toss him out in the garbage as well? With all those recyclables? The karmic debt was getting to me. So I got up and went out to the trashcan. I'd just make sure.

I dug out the box. Past the orange-juice containers. And the milk cartons. It was a little disgusting in there. Still, I found it. And, yep. There were still ashes in the bottom. And boy, was Steve pissed.

"Ell-*ennn*. God. What's the *matter* with you? You stuck me in the trashcan?? You are doing a great job helping Benjamin through this and all, but *pleeease*. This is totally fucked up. Thank you for remembering, I guess. *Je*-sus!"

"Oh, Steve, just shut up, will you?"

I felt like now he was sulking. I'd bought the silver containers. I'd arranged for the scattering. I'd even worried about this enough to come out to the trashcan in the middle of the night. In my night-gown. I'd dug through trash. I don't like bad smells. He knows this. Knew this. He'd been there for that whole recycling debacle. But I'd dug through the bad-smelling trash. He should cut me some slack.

"Look, I'm sorry. But you have no idea how . . . alarming . . . having your ashes around the house has been. SteveMudge is coming this weekend and we are scattering you in the same river where you and Benjamin fished. But now I am going to take this little bit that's left and put it in the garden. Okay?"

He seemed happy about that.

"Oh. In the river. That's good. That's really nice. Way better than the trash."

Okay, he didn't say any of this out loud. I mean, he didn't say it quietly, either. I mean, I know he didn't really *say* it. And I was not losing my mind or anything.

I didn't even say any of my part of the conversation out loud. It was just in my head. I know that.

Not like a hallucination. I wasn't hearing things. It's just. Well. It's hard to explain. He'd been in my dining room, my kitchen, and that closet for a year now. A year. It wears on a person.

I scattered him right then and there in the garden. Well, that little part of him. I can't be specific about which part. Just, you know, a portion of what was left.

Then I double bagged the empty box.

I swear it was now a completely empty box. And I pitched it.

I could not *wait* for trash day. C'mon, trash day.

ooooo

The day that we scattered Steve dawned sunny and clear. We headed to the Mettowee River. The night before, our friend David Silver had come for dinner with Mudge. Two lawyers around the table and they jostled and competed for the air space. SteveMudge is an insurance-industry trial lawyer. He is one of the nation's best. Just ask him.[7]

David Silver is a criminal-defense lawyer. He always has some perfectly honorable guy for a client, who has been wrongly charged with killing his mother and his first-grade teacher before chopping them into pieces and leaving them in Ziplocs in the frozen-food sections of the local grocery stores. The guy is always being framed by the state. As you can imagine.

They had lots to talk about.

Hannah and Dan had come in on the train so they could be here. Eli and Timmy rounded out the room. We had a delicious supper, and the talk flowed with the wine. John had grilled some melt-in-your-mouth buttery sea bass, and I had made a great caesar. A caesar is always fun to make. The thrill of the parboiled egg and making the dressing right in the bowl appeals to my need for a little drama at the table.

There were electric-red beets and garlic scalloped potatoes. Everyone was full and happy. The talk, of course, turned to Steve and fishing. We told David and Timmy and Dan all the stories that they had missed out on by not really knowing him. Steve was always a model human being in the retelling. None of the bad stuff happens in these stories. He was just a loving ex-husband and part of the family.

In bed that night, John and I talked about it.

"Have you noticed how Steve is becoming sort of a saint?" he asked.

John had, of course, been there in the early years. He remem-

---

7. That's not fair. The man doesn't really brag. He just tells lots of colorful stories where he and the juries of Madison County, Illinois, are all heroes.

bered the lawyers and the struggles, as well as the recent years of laughter and love.

"I do. It would probably happen if it were one of us, too," I offered. "But the thing is, you apparently have to die young to qualify."

"Yeah." He thought about it for a second. "I guess it's not a very good trade."

○○○○○

In the morning, we all walked to the river together. It was a sweet spot on Peace Street.[8] There was never anybody there, and it was a beautiful open spot in the woods where the river ran through.

Eli and I had spent countless days there when he was little. We would catch frogs and build rafts. Benjamin and Steve had come to this little shallow spot to fish, too. It was perfect.

Except for the swimmers.

I mean, really? Swimmers!

And two guys with their dogs.

And a bunch of loud, splashing little kids.

You would think these people thought this was a public river, for God's sakes. Good grief.

We waited. The kids and their families seemed to be packing up. But these other people just would not leave. We considered asking them for a little privacy. SteveMudge softly offered to go over and speak to them. But Benjamin was appalled at that.

He seemed suddenly anxious. This was not going according to plan.

So we decided to walk over to the little footbridge and maybe try it from there. The water gushed under the bridge, and we all walked out and sat down, swinging our legs over the edge. Benja-

---

8. Seriously.

min had an old Viking blessing that he wanted to read saved on his phone,[9] only he couldn't get service for long enough to pull it up. The anxiety was palpable as he searched.

So to break the tension, I told a story about the time Steve and I had gone on a float trip. We had both told this story for years. Steve loved the water. We'd gone with a bunch of his coworkers from Newhard Cook on a float trip. We were in a canoe and Steve had been giving me direction all day. We'd only been married for about fifteen minutes, and this was at minute twelve or so. Not our glory days. At one point he had stood up in the bow of the canoe and held his oar over his head, pretending to be a Viking.

It *was* pretty funny, actually.

Only, then we hit the rapids.

"Ell-*ennn!!!!!* Ellen, paddle to the right . . . Ell-*ennn!!* . . . El—"

The next thing I knew, everything was in the water.[10]

Steve went flying out headfirst. It looked pretty dangerous. Everyone on the trip was concerned. We all were scanning the water. Nothing. No Steve.

Then he popped up spitting water and sputtering, "God-*damnit* Ellen!"

Well, I got in somebody else's canoe for the rest of the trip.

His friends called me Goddamnit from that day forward. You know, as in, "Hey Goddamnit, could you please pass the pepper?"

At Steve's funeral, a long-ago acquaintance introduced herself and tentatively said, "Goddamnit?"

We both doubled over laughing.

---

9. Steve had gone through a genealogy phase, where he was sure he'd turned up proof that he had descended from the Vikings. Well, why not?

10. Except for me. I had somehow managed to come through upright and unscathed.

"So I know Steve would want to be in the water. Just like any good Viking would."

Benjamin gave up and said, "Let's just do it."

So I opened the big vessel we'd brought along. I'd kept one smaller one for Mindy and a little one for Benjamin just in case. I handed it to him. He grabbed a handful of ash and tossed it into the water. Steve made white, cloudy swirls that danced and bubbled and twirled along the river.

Benjamin passed the container down, and each of us, Eli, Hannah, Dan, John, me, and SteveMudge, took a turn. Back at last in Benjamin's hands, he emptied the rest. With tears streaming down our cheeks, we watched Steve, or what had been Steve, swirl away. It was beautiful, really.

I imagined Steve Stimson sitting right alongside us.

"Way better than the trashcan, Steve. You were right," I thought.

I figured I could let him win this argument.

He was crying, too.

"I know. This was really beautiful. Thank you Ellen . . ."

But not out loud.

I swear.

ooooo

On the way back, Benjamin threw his dad's line into the water and we all watched him cast. It took about fifteen minutes, but sure enough he reeled in a fish. He shouted up at us from the middle of the river with a big grin.

"In honor of Steve!" And then he let it go.

In honor of Steve.

ooooo

MAKING ROOM

Steve had said, "I think I'd make a nice centerpiece. That silver vessel you got for me is real pretty."

No, of course he didn't actually say it. But, as I pictured an empty chair at the table last Thanksgiving, I could easily imagine how he might have liked me to solve it. But I'd already burned one table and I didn't like the symmetry of putting any more ashes on that one ever.

One of the underappreciated things about the wrought iron tables outside is that they don't burn. They don't put that in brochures, but maybe they should. Alas, it would be too cold to sit out on the terrace for Thanksgiving. It did give me an idea, though.

We had a bunch of small metal tables that we used on the terrace for big parties. There was the main wrought-iron table that sat out there for most of the year that accommodated eight comfortably. With the four smaller ones, we could add another sixteen people for a really festive outdoor party. And I started to imagine bringing those tables into the library and draping them with long gypsy tablecloths, putting them in the middle of the room. If it was cold, we could even have a fireside dinner.

And that is how library meals came into our lives.

There haven't been too many . . . a couple of brunches, a Christmas dinner, and always at parties there is a long table with hors d'oeuvres for the cocktail hour or pastries for dessert. Bringing the tables into the library changes everything. It is like hanging a banner that says FESTIVAL over the door. With a cheery fire there is an intimacy and sense of celebration we don't get at any other table. The library is the place to toast a big, happy thing. It is also the place to mourn a lost member of the family.

Champagne goes with the library. So does soup in a homemade bread bowl beside the fire. It is a place for extra celebration or gentle tending. The library is one of the warmest spots in the house, and in summer it's one of the sunniest. With its deep red walls, high, glossy, painted-tin ceilings, marble-wrapped fireplace, and mantel festooned with bits of seasonal beauty, it is a room that demands and gives attention.

Now it is another place where we can feed ourselves. We cover up sad memories by making new ones.

At the table. Always at the table.

CHAPTER TEN

Still Alive

It was September, and already there was an occasional bite of fall in the air. We were planning a bonfire party to kick off the season. There would be steak sandwiches with balsamic onions alongside piles of french fries. Caramel apples for dessert. Maybe we could do s'mores around the bonfire, too, if people stayed late enough.

Eli was back in school, but everything was different this time around. After he'd had a pretty good year at Burr and Burton, we read about the opening of the academy's Mountain Campus. It was about twenty miles outside town in Peru, Vermont. They were offering a semester-long humanitas program built around sustainability. The description sounded nice. "Building and organizing a culture of sustainability, learning how to build sustainable economic social healthy life support for everyone that shares our planet." That sounded like something I could get behind.[1]

The Mountain Campus building was impossibly gorgeous. It looked like maybe Disney had been in on the design. The scale was grand, for one thing, and for another, it looked like the image that comes to mind when you think "mountain retreat." There were giant tree-trunk beams alongside trees as supports. There was a fireplace with a slate chimney, lofted thirty-foot ceilings, and glass everywhere looking out into the woods.

The idea behind the campus was for the kids to learn first-

---

1. The whole little recycling problem notwithstanding.

hand what it means to live well in this place. The history courses would focus on the land around them. Their literature would consist of adventure stories about mountain life. This hands-on experience would include several camping and hiking trips. There would be time for quiet reflection once every week in their own private Dakinas.

For his admissions application, Eli and his brother had made an autobiographical short film. He talked about being a hands-on learner. It was an affecting microdocumentary that captured his warm personality. When John and I watched it, we figured he'd get in. And sure enough, he did. We thought that with all the recent memory problems, this was a great answer to the learning challenges he was facing.

But as the first day of school neared, Eli had second thoughts.

"I think maybe we made a mistake. Do you guys know that I hate camping?"

And as any good mom would, I responded with, "How do you know, honey? You've never tried it."[2]

"Well, exactly." Eli was glad that we seemed to recognize the value of his argument. "We stay at the W. With room service. I'm thinking there won't be room service under a tarp in the woods. What do you think?" A reasoned, mature argument. He was feeling confident enough to add in additional points like, "Also, I hate the cold."

"Eli! You are so lucky, man," Benjamin chimed in. "You are going to love this. Besides, you and Timmy practically lived outside when you were younger. I wish I could have done something like this in high school." And then he went in for the most persuasive argument he could imagine for a teenager. "Just think. You probably won't even have homework. How bad can it be?"

---

2. The "thank you" taste is the refuge of moms everywhere. "Come on, sweetie. Just take a 'thank you' taste for me."

Benjamin had made that admission movie, and he was totally onboard. He was at the house picking up Olive, who had been visiting us while he was ocean fishing one last time on the island for the season. Turns out, Steve had left saltwater rods, too. Rods he'd apparently purchased, you know, just in case.

Benjamin was just in the door, practically. He had a bunch of stories, and could hardly sit still.

"Next year, I think I am going to buy a boat. I want to chase those false albacores next summer. The bonita are calling my name. God, I love this so much. I wonder why Steve never went ocean fishing?" It was essentially one sentence. Practically one breath.

He had just finished the best trout-fishing season in the whole history of trout, to hear him tell it. In local shallow streams, the kid was catching rainbow trout that were over a foot long. Sixteen and seventeen inches, in fact. Apparently this was amazing. He had said at least a hundred times that he was living *A River Runs Through It* right in his backyard. He had the pictures to prove it.

Steve's ashes had taken on an almost mystical quality at this point. Benjamin had this kind of secret theory that the reason he was catching so many huge fish had something to do with those ashes. It was as if his dad had blessed the river somehow. Now, we also knew that New England was dealing with the weird aftermath of Hurricane Irene, which had churned everything up in new and unexpected ways. And that the prior winter had been the mildest on record in Vermont. That meant that many creatures bred early and lived longer this year. These were just details, though. Barely "facts."

Alongside those facts were two other details. We had scattered Steve's ashes in Benjamin's river. Steve, the great fly-fisherman. And now, Benjamin was catching giant fish in streams that were six inches deep. Streams that the locals swore hadn't seen fish for years. Believe what you want.

But here in the kitchen, Eli was still complaining.

"Sure, great. You just had the best fishing of your life on a nice warm sandy beach, and I am about to be camping in minus-ten-degree weather." The sarcasm was . . . chilly.

"Eli, it is September."

"It won't be for long." Well, he had us there. But John and I are the parents, and even if Benjamin couldn't help us win over Eli on the basis of persuasion, we still got to decide.

Before long, October had come and the kid was settled in. In fact, he loved it. He and Benjamin would swap woodsy stories at least once a week over dinner.

One day we heard about ferns. Who knew that a teenage boy could get excited about ferns? Another night, it was caves.

"Yesterday we went through a marble cavern. Ohmygod. There is a whole nother world just under our feet. There is so much we don't know."

His imagination had been rekindled. It was a great relief. School didn't have to be a source of pain.

And now our family had two fishermen. Eli had taken up fishing again over the summer at the pond. With his renewed outdoor life at the Mountain Campus, he was fishing in Vermont. The anxiety he had been living with had passed. It had been replaced by the thrill of feeling competent again.

The outdoor world was different from the school world he had been disappointed by. This was a world where rote memorization didn't matter. It was a world where the marks on the trees told you a story. You just had to look at them to remember. The semester had already been so good for Eli that he had let us persuade him to consider some kind of similar gap-year program after high school and before college. We just wanted to buy him time to deal with this brain thing.

It was too bad that the Mountain Campus experience was only for one semester. We had no idea what we would do when January came. But for now . . . for now, everyone in this family was feeling whole again.

ooooo

Christmas has always been a big part of the glue for our family. It is a time filled with warm memories and big fun. Our family traditions are many, and they give us all deep pleasure. And after the year we'd been having, Christmas Adventure seemed even more important than usual.

Since our first year together as a family, John and I have returned to that first Christmas as the template for Christmas Adventure. We no longer go to Famous-Barr and listen to Andy Williams piped over the music system as we ride the escalators, but the basics are still there. There's a big dinner, an overnight stay in a hotel, and new ornaments. Steve might have come over at the end to help us trim the tree and drink some eggnog. He even contributed a few ornaments over the years. After twenty-three years of Christmas Adventure, this one might be a little different.

Generally, it's just us on the Adventures. One year, though, we invited Aunt Patsy. Patricia is an old friend, and she met us for a dinner on Adventure weekend one year in New York City. We had such a good time. She's been invited to at least a meal during Adventure every year since.[3]

We headed to New York this year and were staying downtown at our favorite W Hotel in Union Square. I had gobs of Starwood

---

3. Aunt Patsy is Patricia Bostelman, who is the least "Patsy" person you will ever meet. A brilliant, Armani-wearing city girl. A young Hannah nicknamed her Aunt Patsy, and in a family-wide fit of irony, it stuck. We love her, and unaccountably, she loves all of us back.

points saved up from work, and this always feels like the perfect way to spend them. Union Square is a great place to be at Christmastime too. Eli likes to run out for a slice of pizza just up the street. Hannah loves the Union Square Christmas Market, where there are always cute little coats for Pippi and warm gingerbread and hot cocoa for us while we walk aimlessly from stall to stall. Benjamin likes Rothman's, the men's store across the square, where Robert Graham shirts and cool jeans can be had. Even for the tall guys. And John and I love it all.

We walked down to Madison Square and checked out Eataly, Mario Batali's new food concept. It's a city block that is gourmet grocer, gelateria, wine shop, and truffle bar under one bustling roof. We wandered into Max Brenner (Chocolate By the Bald Man) for the best spicy Mexican hot cocoa. We love the smells of the food carts and the sounds of the musical performers in the square. We hold hands and feel the energy of the city under our feet.

ABC Carpet and Home often has the best ornaments for us. After all these years, we still get one new ornament each on Adventure weekend. Our tree is heavy with the bounty of years gone by.

The tree is a place where we tell lots of stories. Eli had a phase where he only wanted the biggest, most Christmasy bauble he could find. It needed to be screaming, "I AM an Ornament!" No subtlety allowed. But there are also lots of lovely colorful bits of German spun glass on the tree. Hannah always chooses animals. I choose mainly Santas and wintery little houses. John picks the goofy stuff. He might choose a pudding-pop-eating polar bear or an ice-skating penguin. Benjamin tends to pick something related to his interests that year. Batman memorabilia and fishing lures have been common.

Our tree is my favorite thing. In a fire, it is the ornaments I would want to save. They tell the story of our lives. There is the little orange Christmas tree Benjamin made when he was five. Orange was his favorite color, so the tree had to be orange. Of course. Eli's contributions are fantastical and huge. Hannah's ornaments are a menagerie of kittens and dolphins and bears and birds. This tree is like the crest of our clan. It is loud and colorful. It makes me believe in us every year all over again.

At the end of the day, though, we head back to the W. When you walk through the doors, you can recognize that you've made it to the right place by the music. The lights in the lobby are dim and the music is a slightly-too-loud techno-pop beat. It is way hip. Our kids love it. Really, so do we.

We got on the elevators after a long wandering Saturday, and immediately one of us embarrassed our kids nearly to death. It wasn't the one you might think this time, either. Now, at the W, guests have to use room keys to unlock the security block to access the upper floors. Naturally we were all digging around in our wallets and purses for the keys that we'd had "just a minute ago." No keys. And, really, that beat was so incessant you couldn't think. So of course John did the only reasonable thing. He started dancing.

Well, I say dancing. It is hard to describe this . . . movement . . . as dancing. Per se. His head was sort of jutting out and back. An epileptic-turtle move, if you can imagine. And his arms were out at his sides doing a similar thrusting motion. Kind of a smooth version of the Robot . . . Epileptic Turtle with Smooth Robot Arms. Oh, and he was totally rockin' the beat.

"*Da-ad!*" I'd credit it, but I'm sure that each of the kids offered some mortified version of it at the same time.

"I am not Da-ad. I am Hipstah Da-ad," John replied, and kept right on jutting and thrusting.

He started adding in sounds, because really what this whole show was missing was more of a soundtrack. There were clicks and whooshes, which were suddenly punctuated by a *Wheeeeee!* whistling sound.

We were all cracking up. Hipstah Dad knew his audience. But of course this wasn't getting us any closer to our rooms. Finally Eli opened the elevator door, since we could not find a single damned key. We needed to go back to the front desk to get a new batch.

And there stood a row of those actual honest-to-God-hip W employees staring down at monitors and laughing their asses off, in their fashionably black uniforms. Apparently, and you might not know this, but apparently elevators have security cameras. John was clearly the evening's entertainment.

The front-desk staff had called in employees from other parts of the building to take a look. There was pointing, and a few attempts to mimic the whoosh and whistle of Hipstah Dad. For my money, the original was better.

"Umm. Huh," was all Benjamin could offer.

Eli moaned.

Hannah gave a heartfelt "Ohmygod!"

John and I just laughed, as the row of very young black-clad designer-hotel employees looked up and grinned at all of us. I had the impression that we were their favorite guests. Now and forever.

When we got back to the elevators with new keys in hand, Hannah and Eli pushed the "door close" button and waited patiently till we reached our floor.

With keys.

Inside the elevator. Standing quietly.

John began the performance.

Be boppa boppah be boppa boppah shewwwheeeeee!

Eli didn't speak to us for an hour.

ooooo

This is the type of thing that we would have shared with Steve. He didn't always come on Christmas Adventure. Since we'd moved to

Vermont, it wasn't easy for him to be there for the tree trimming. We would usually skype, though. Steve loved gadgets, so he would want to be able to use Skype to talk to us all. Of course, that didn't always work as easily as it sounded like it should.

Last year he'd bought a new laptop with a camera feature. We spent the whole conversation staring at his chest. But he would have liked to have seen Hipstah Dad.

This Christmas, though, there would be no skyping with Steve. We had his laptop.

And besides, he doesn't have very good Wi-Fi where he is now.

○○○○○

In Vermont, Christmas is always an especial pleasure. It comes complete with sparkly snow and wood smoke.[4] We go to New York for the Adventure, but we come right back and find the biggest tree John thinks might fit through the door of our house. Every year, I want bigger and he lobbies for smaller. We wander through rows of snow-tipped branches and make sure the one we picked doesn't have a nest of winter birds snuggled in.

This year the tree was about ten feet tall. It fit. Don't let him try to tell you otherwise.

It fit.

And this year we have Elsie. Elsie is Hannah and Dan's six-month-old Great Dane puppy.

Yes, that's right. Great. Dane.

Don't get me started on this.

Hannah and Dan live together in New York. They weren't completely happy with their apartment, and besides, the rent had

---

4. "Over the river and through the woods" must have been written with a
   Vermont Christmas in mind.

been going up this year. Also, Hannah desperately missed having a dog. I mean, she has Pippi, but Pippi lives with us. And over the years, Pippi has settled in here. It seemed unfair to move her to New York. She's a Vermont dog accustomed to snow and woods and her pack. So, anyway, Hannah started looking for a new place. A new apartment that would take dogs. She called me one day saying,

"Oh, Mommy![5] We have found the perfect apartment!!" She was delighted. "It has slate counter tops *and* a washer and dryer,[6] a dishwasher,[7] and two balconies!

"It was a home for tuberculosis patients at the turn of the century, so every apartment has at least one balcony and ours has two! Plus, oh God, it even has exposed brick walls and they take dogs!!!!!"

All the exclamation points are necessary. She might have been hyperventilating. One minor, hardly worth mentioning, really, detail about the place. Well, two.

First, it cost *more* than the apartment they were leaving. The apartment that they were leaving because the rent was going up. Of course.

And, it was a sixth-floor walkup.

She kept saying "puppy" and "balconies" in breathless sentence fragments, like only young women in their twenties can. And I kept thinking:

Six.

Floors.

And . . .

Puppy.

---

5. I am always Mommy at times of great distress or great happiness.

6. Which are apparently like gold in Manhattan.

7. More gold.

Turned out they had already paid the deposit. They were moving.

Then, they got the puppy.

A Great Dane puppy. In a sixth-floor walkup.[8]

ooooo

Elsie is a lovely dog. She's adorable. And we love our granddogs. But she was also a puppy. A very big puppy. A puppy who then, of course, got diarrhea.

Hannah brought Elsie to stay with us for two weeks, because a twenty-five-pound infant with diarrhea doesn't really work with six flights of stairs. Hannah and Dan would take her outside to do her business, and The Baby would poop. All the way down six flights. On everything. Everything. Before they got out the door.

Hannah and Elsie came to visit for a good long while. I'm not sure whether the neighbors kicked in gas money to encourage the extended stay.

ooooo

So, this Christmas, we have a gorgeous ten-foot-tall tree[9] and a giant rambunctious puppy with the tiniest little digestive trouble. With Hannah's bunny LuLu and Benjamin's Olive, we will have twenty-eight paws in the house this Christmas.

That sounds about right, I think.

Already under our tree is a beautiful handmade fly rod from Benjamin to Eli. I sneaked and read the card:

---

8. I figured she would at least have the best legs in the city by the time it was all over.

9. It really did fit through the door.

I've been waiting a long time for you to find fishing on your own. Now that you have, it's time for me to step in. Most people begin fishing with spinning gear. I know I did. But as we evolve so does our fishing. In this family, we fish with rods, not poles. I hope you love you're new axe, buddy. Can't wait to fish it with you.

I cried. Well, of course I did.

ooooo

We will probably go on a sleigh ride this year when the snow gets deep. Vermont has horse-drawn sleighs that will come to your house and ride you around under a sky full of winter stars. We always find the Big Dipper and the North Star first. And pretty soon we are hunting for Rigel.

Orion is the Hunter of the skies, and tucked within Orion is one of the five brightest stars visible from Vermont. Rigel is a whopping 770 light years away. It is tucked into the foot of Orion. *Rigel* is Arabic for foot.

Seven hundred and seventy light years. It is like our very own secret. What it seems to come down to when you are looking up and imagining all that time is the same thing. It's the same thing that you decided mattered when you were listening to that old transistor radio at fifteen. The essence of the "whole thing" seems to be love.

Just like every good preacher says, our job in this world is to do as much of that loving as we possibly can with the time we have and with the people who are on the ride with us. I would add a corollary. We should also have as much fun doing it as we possibly can. I think we are supposed to choose people to ride with us, too. For me, that is one of the main points of the whole exercise. Pick a pack and love them up.

Our pack includes a gun-toting fly-fishing filmmaker, a skate-boarding hat-wearing ball-twirling teenager, a brainy funny woman who loves animals, children, and every sunny beach near a good restaurant. There's also a music-loving intellectual and his wife, a fast-moving mountain-loving business gypsy. And the two of us have been reading and talking for almost a quarter of a century. I am just impossibly grateful about that.

We have a city aunt, who gives smart, thoughtful advice to all of us, a small-town aunt who calls and listens to every story every kid wants to tell always and forever and loves all of us no matter what, one live-in city boyfriend who unaccountably loves the Jets,[10] a quirky bunch of Vermont pals,[11] and a few far-flung people who give us movies to watch and books to read and friendship across the miles. We love all these people and they, thankfully, love us right back,

And we will always remember one former husband/dad/uncle/friend, who loved safari clothes and good equipment.

You know, it doesn't matter that your hips may be too wide, or that your family configuration is . . . weird.

Because it turns out, we just don't have that kind of time.

ooooo

---

10. Oh, and the Rangers, and the Knicks, and . . . well, you get the idea.

11. An artist who interprets our dreams, an inventor who might save you with a rubber band, a stick, and a little glue, a woman who really should run her own country and is more sister to me than any blood relative could ever be, and a brainy guy who laconically solves every puzzle.

THE COUNTER

In our kitchen, there is an old pharmacist's counter. It is long and curved, nicked and scratched. It is walnut, oak, and pine. It looks like it belongs right in that kitchen, as if it has always been there. One neighbor told us that a pharmacist used to live here and that he had used it for dispensing medicines right out of our kitchen. When we came to this house, the counter was in the basement covered by dozens of years of dirt. We cleaned it, and intuitively we stuck it right back in the place where it probably began its life.

That counter is a grand old thing with deep cabinets and drawers. One end is where we cut and chop and mix and roll. The long part in the middle was just made for a lazy holiday buffet. We fill it with platters of ham and loaves of crusty bread. There is usually a giant bowl of pimento cheese and hot ramekins filled with gooey mac 'n' cheese, alongside garlicky tenderloins on dollar rolls with a bit of blue cheese and maybe a drop of balsamic. On Christmas morning after the nut roll and presents under the tree, John and I make our way into the kitchen and cook for a couple of hours. Then we haul out all the red platters and fill the counter with more food than any of us could possibly eat. The kids often have friends who drop by. And so do we. Everyone meanders in and out and nibbles all through the day in between new books and backgammon tournaments around the table. The dogs all have new bones and pig's ears, so the counter doesn't even get their attention. Even Sadie the Bengal ignores the tenderloin in favor of the catnip Santa left her under the tree.

The counter is for snacking. Piled high with delicious treats, it is the place where we can grab and go. At least once a week, I scrub and oil it, rubbing deeply into all of the cracks. In between, it gets generous slatherings of olive oil, so it always feels supple and warm. The counter is old. And strong. All the scratches and gouges give it a special character and beauty that it never could have had when it was brand-new. I think Vermont could have an earthquake and that counter would still be standing right where it is . . . where it almost always has. I take sweet comfort in that. My counter. I guess we all probably do.

CHAPTER ELEVEN

Good Grief

Journal Entry: 2011
Written at the kitchen table.

Grief is a lot like arthritis. The first time you notice the pain in your toe or your back or your knees you run to the doctor.

You are in pain.

You hurt.

You must have an injury. You tell people about it and they furrow their brow and describe a time when they experienced something similar. You think back repeatedly to what you might have done wrong. Did you twist it? Maybe it was all that driving. What could you have done differently? Everyone has an idea about what you should do. You need a prescription or maybe a sling.

Only then your doctor asks you how old you are. What has that got to do with anything, you wonder? X-rays are ordered. You are thinking that really an MRI is what is needed. You have boutique healthcare so you get one of those, too. The verdict comes back, and again, someone asks how old you are. You wonder why all these twelve-year-old doctors are obsessed with your age. Then someone says the word. Arthritis.

What? Wait. You are in your forties. Arthritis is something old people get. Like your grandmother who had to stop quilting because of it. You are young. You are hip, dammit. You wear 7 for All Mankind blue jeans. What the hell is wrong with these people?

Eventually the notion begins to settle in and you realize that there are fancy drugs for this. They all have side effects. There is, also, the old reliable bottle of Motrin.

It helps. A little.

You are stiffer in the mornings, so you get in the hot tub while you have your coffee. Or perhaps you sign up for yoga. The pain can seem a little worse when you're not preoccupied somewhere else. Your doctor seems unconcerned. You stop talking about it because you are not going to be one of those people who discuss their medical issues. You are not. Those people are boring. You are going to talk about politics and art until you are ninety. Not what hurts.

And this is, after all, a common ailment. You learn how to mitigate it, stretch, swallow an anti-inflammatory, and get on with your day. It is no longer shocking. Pretty soon it becomes white noise. It is in the background. It is there, but like with your awkward cowlick or ample backside, you make room, move over and accommodate it. Grief becomes a part of your life. And eventually it stops hurting in the way you think of as "pain."

It is quieter and only sometimes flares up and makes noise. Sometimes on warm days, you don't feel it at all. You remember happy things or funny times and no sharp pain hits you in the ribs. Grief is a companion. Remember how romantic love showed up in your teens and turned you inside out? It took years to learn how to do that without being Nutsy Fagan all the time. Grief is a little like that. It is big, and eventually you learn how to make room.

ooooo

I was no longer shocked that Steve wouldn't be at Hannah's graduation. We had Olive now. And Hannah's Dan, too. Life keeps moving forward. As it always does. Steve was far too young and we weren't ready. Benjamin, of course, least of all. I did not expect to be teaching my kids how to cope with the loss of their parent. I figured I would die first. Well, okay, Steve was older and so I guess I figured when we were old, he would probably die first. But the "when we were old" was a key part of the equation. Benjamin would be married with kids of his own.

That timetable was surely blown. And now, we were left to figure it out on our own. This was such a loss. Steve was part of our real family. He loved us all madly, and he had finally gotten to a place where he was sort of easy with himself. He could laugh at the things that once drove him crazy. He adored me and Hannah. He was proud of Benjamin, who he worried about all the time. He loved him fiercely, most of all, I think, and that was his most uneven relationship. He got a huge kick out of Eli, and John was his friend. His fifties were his best decade.

I miss his emails. I cannot believe he will not get to come to the Vineyard with us this summer. We should have done it last year.

The lesson, as if we needed reminding, has been loud. Live with intention. Live on purpose. Every day.

ooooo

Journal Entry: 2011, continued
Thank God for Olive.

I need to make some art.

Maybe I'll write a book.

We should all go to Morocco.

I think I'll encourage Hannah to live on the beach with Dan this summer. Who cares? She needs to have more fun.

John and I should have more sex outside. He is the sexiest man I know. We used to love doing it in the grass. We'll just take thicker, soft blankets or something.

I wish he'd take up an instrument.

I'll bring it up. And Eli can become a professional skateboarder for all I care. Nobody is going to make him hurry. There is nothing wrong with being a late bloomer. He is young. It is not a fucking race.

BEDSIDE

My bedside table is a shabby old turquoise. It usually has some candles and a pile of books on top. It also has three little drawers. In the second one, there is a compact disc with a picture of Steve on the cover. It is the slide show from his memorial service. Next to that is a little leather notebook that was in his car on the shelf under his radio. It is full of lists he made, like this one:

- *Lunch in Paris* by Elizabeth Bard
- Camp Oil
- *Fishers of Men* by Adam Elenbaas
- Fire starter fluid
- C batteries
- Barba Roja Barrel-
  Aged Red Ale
  $12 for 750 ml
  from BarbaraJa Argentina
  Rated 91
- English muffins

Epilogue

THOSE LITTLE NOTEBOOKS OF STEVE'S WERE SCATTERED ALL over his house. There is another small one in my drawer that has lists of names for his future house and even more books he'd planned to read.

I can't say why these particular journals spoke to me over the others that he kept. Or even why they are in my bedside-table drawer. I don't look at them often. I looked at them when we first went to his house after he died and then again when I came home. And once more just now. But I like having them. When I am fumbling in the dark sometimes I forget they are there. My hand brushes the leather and I feel a sweet fleeting connection.

It is not as if these are the trinkets saved from an old lover. They are that, I suppose. But he was my lover for a much shorter time than he was everything else, so that is not a part I even remember clearly.

A month or two after Steve died I was talking about the head-aches that I had not completely solved and how maybe they were tied to the grief. A friend at dinner looked astonished that I would speak in loving terms about grieving "your ex-husband!?," he exclaimed with a raised eye and a jokey-sorrowful look at John.

I didn't get it.

Ex-husband? Well, sort of. More, he was the father of my child. He had been a great enemy years before and wound up my great friend. Ex-husband. What a silly, limiting term that is.

It would not have ever occurred to John to mind. Or to me to be careful about it either. This was a relationship we all shared. Steve was family. Sometimes you keep the family you are born with and sometimes you make up a new one as you go along. Steve was a part of my real family . . . the one that John and I have built together, memory by memory.

I have said that grief is like living with an old familiar pain. But also . . . eventually . . . it is like living with an old familiar love. It turns out, unsurprisingly, once you think hard about it, that it is the love we keep. The leather journals are a physical manifestation of that love. It is a warm feeling. There were days just after Steve died when we all stayed in our jammies and ate soup and moped. I think that was mourning.

But this table and now this drawer, this little representation of a life, this is grief. Benjamin wears one of his dad's hunting jackets. That is another living representation of grief. There is a contentment to this grown-up grief. Grown-up grief has been around a while. It is not so raw, and it is, almost, a comfort. When Hannah graduated from college we all imagined Steve tearing up and saying, as he had said a thousand times before,

"That's our Ivy League girl. Hannah, I am so proud of you."

Mount Holyoke is one of the Seven Sisters, the first, but still, not quite an Ivy. Just try telling Steve that, though.

And when I chose the pictures of Steve for his memorial slide show, I imagined him saying, "Oh, Ellen, for God's sake, do you have to put that one in? *Je*-sus."

And then I put it in anyway.

Just like I would have done if he'd been alive to argue with me over it.

And of Olive and Benjamin, we now know he would have filled many albums of proud pictures. Steve would have compared her to his dog, Lady. Every dog got compared to his Lady.

This is grief. A year and a half in. Good grief. It is company now.

Part of us. Part of the story of our family.

We all learned about it together. And so because of it, and because of Steve, I know that if John dies right after we have a fight about how he never changes a single damned light bulb and would live in the dark if I died first . . . I won't mind. Because what I know is that we have had a loving, joyful, and full life together. I have been his good wife and he has been my good husband. Light bulbs notwithstanding.

The last moment is no more important than the one before that. It is a life. My kids know this, too. Because I have told them. If they have just told me how I embarrassed them for the sixty-seventh time and couldn't I please just this once behave myself, and then I die— they are not to worry. Because, first they gave me years of pleasure and love. The messes and complaints are just part of that whole.

Grief is just another one of the stories we can tell now. We try to tell it with joy and laughter. I feel lucky to know grief in this close and intimate way. It was the last present Steve gave to our family. Turns out we were a parenting team in this way, too. And I will always be grateful for it.

Acknowledgments

Rosalie Siegel, my beloved and esteemed agent, who got it all rolling. Todd Porter, who makes everything better. Kermit Hummel and Bill Rusin, authentic bookmen. Lisa Sacks, Tom Haushalter, and Melissa Dobson—the mistakes are mine and the improvements invariably theirs. I am impossibly grateful to all of you.

Most especially, big loud messy love and thanks to my John, Benjamin, Hannah, and Eli for generously letting me tell our stories. Not to mention always giving me such great material . . .